300 YEARS
AGO TODAY

300 YEARS AGO TODAY

A Beginner's Guide to the Union of 1707

Paul Riddell

THE SALTIRE SOCIETY

300 Years Ago Today published 2009 by

The Saltire Society
9 Fountain Close,
22 High Street,
Edinburgh EH1 1TF

A catalogue record for this book is available
from the British Library.

ISBN 978 0854111 046

Cover Design by James Hutcheson

Printed and Bound in Scotland by Bell and Bain Limited

Preface

In late September of 2006 the then Editor of *The Scotsman*, Mike Gilson, asked me to come up with some ideas on how the paper could mark the tercentenary of the Act of Union. Newly-arrived from the south coast of England, he was excited by the coincidence of such a significant anniversary in Scottish history and an election just over three months later that the Scottish National Party appeared likely to win. One of my suggestions was the series of articles out of which this short book has grown.

The idea was a refinement of one of the oldest (and easiest) methods newspapers use to fill column inches: taking a look back in the archives. In this case, of course, the situation was complicated by the fact that *The Scotsman* did not exist until 1817. Unfortunately, the archives of the newspaper that did exist, *The Edinburgh Courant*, were unavailable at the National Library. So I had to fall back on original documents, memoirs and the extensive historiography of the period. The latter was very timeously brought right up to date just as I was embarking on the project with the publication of Professor Christopher Whatley's magisterial *The Scots and the Union*, Michael Fry's *The Union*, and Paul H. Scott's *The Union of 1707: Why and How*.

My intention had been to give a precise account of the goings on "on that day" 300 years previously; sometimes, alas, the answer was "not very much" (a surprisingly common refrain even now in the era of 24-hour rolling news). That allowed me to include several character sketches and paint in some of the historical background without which it is impossible fully to understand the period.

Gratifyingly, the response from our readers was wholly positive, demonstrating that there is a great deal of interest in Scottish history among the general public. I was flattered to be told by one history lecturer that she had used some of my pieces to help introduce her students to the subject. An introduction to the subject is what this book is intended to be. Readers keen to see for themselves the key historical venues, or their modern manifestations, will find a short guide at the end of the book.

Researching and writing an article every day for four months, at the same time as doing the "day job", turned out to be a Sisyphean labour. I'd like to thank Mike for allowing me the time to do the series justice. Among other colleagues, I would like to single out Bill Jamieson and George Kerevan for sharing their wisdom so liberally and Bob Thomson who sub-edited most of these pieces brilliantly and therefore saved me from the embarrassment of countless errors. I am indebted also to Chris Whatley and Paul Scott for their advice.

Thanks are due to the Royal Society of Edinburgh, whose members I was invited to address as part of a conference on the Union in May 2007. The talk I gave there forms the basis of my introduction.

Graham High kindly agreed to produce a series of excellent cartoons that with Hogarthian humour help to bring the era alive.

Finally, special mention must be made of Ian Scott of the Saltire Society, whose idea this book was and with whom I have found it a great pleasure to work.

This book is dedicated to my wife Ruth and our son Magnus.

PR
Edinburgh 2008

Contents

1

INTRODUCTION

"Politics is not the art of the possible," wrote the economist John Kenneth Galbraith to President John F. Kennedy in 1962, in conscious denial of Bismarck's celebrated claim. Rather, Galbraith observed, "It consists in choosing between the disastrous and the unpalatable." For me this neatly sums up the predicament facing Scotland's politicians in Edinburgh in 1706. And let us remember that, contrary to the tenor of much of the current discussion surrounding these events, it *was* up to the Scottish Parliament whether to approve the Articles of Union. MPs had a choice.

We journalists like to poke our noses into things, present and past, so I want to attempt to take you, dear reader, on a journey back to the Edinburgh of the early eighteenth century. As a thought experiment I'd like you to try to lay aside everything you know about what happened after 1707. For truly to understand the motivations of those whom Burns accused of having been "bought and sold for English gold", we must rid ourselves of the bias of hindsight – and try to place ourselves at the heart of events in the tumultuous late seventeenth and early eighteenth centuries. It is also important to retain a sense of Realpolitik – of the international situation in an age of ferocious great power politics. Only then is it possible to challenge the woolly thinking that governs some of the modern-day analysis of this period of our history.

Begin by imagining yourself as a disinterested observer in Parliament Hall, home of the Scottish Parliament, in, say, late October 1706. Apart from the obvious physical differences – perruque wigs, robes, swords (and the stench outside) – after a little inquiry you would immediately be struck by two things:

(i) The extent to which the nobility or aristocracy – Hamilton, Queensberry, Argyll, Atholl (a "bristling collection of superegos"[1] if ever there was one) – dominated proceedings. Out of a total membership of 223, 68 were Lords, but their influence was far greater than the arithmetic suggests.

(ii) The extremely narrow franchise on which the remaining two estates – barons or shire representatives and burgh representatives – had been elected. (Midlothian, which had 100 voters, is deemed to have had the largest electorate.[2])

Beyond Parliament Hall, you would have encountered what the English spy and journalist Daniel Defoe called the "rabble", or the mob. "We have two mobs since my last [letter]," he wrote to his paymaster Sir Robert Harley, English Secretary of State. "But we had the last two nights a worse mob than this . . . and certainly a Scots rabble is the worst of its kind . . . I went up the street in a friend's coach in the evening, and some of the mob not then got together were heard to say when I went into a house, 'There was one of the English dogs etc.'"[3] (Note that little bit of journalistic licence – "were heard to say".) Xenophobic feeling was running high – on both sides of the border. But the mob wasn't the only source of opinion. There were pamphlets and mass petitions galore. As Dr Karin Bowie says in her splendid book on Scottish public opinion and the Union, "The scale of popular involvement was remarkable for the time."[4]

Consider also for a moment the issue of sovereignty. It is one the most contested in Scottish history; it still is today. For me, sovereignty is simply the "possession of ultimate legal authority"[5], which lay in Scotland in 1706 with Queen Anne as monarch in association – *yes* with the English Parliament, but *also* with the Scottish Parliament.

In 1603 James VI had gone to London to take the throne of England following the death of his cousin Elizabeth I, who had executed his mother, Mary Queen of Scots. "Here I sit and governe it [Scotland] with my pen . . . which others could not do by the sword," he said,[6] and he was right. Yet James, fervent believer in divine right though he was, failed to turn the Union of the Crowns into a parliamentary union.

When James's grandson, King James VII and II, was deposed by William of Orange in the Revolution of 1688-89, the notion of the divine right of monarchs began to crumble. John Locke, in his *Two Treatises of Government*, advocated the concept of the consent of the governed. William submitted to rule in tandem with a more assertive English Parliament. In Scotland, a separate pact was made, and William was accepted as King through the Claim of Right in 1690. Soon afterwards, the Presbyterian Church of Scotland was ratified as the national church, with the monarch as a member, not as its head. And the Lords of the Articles, the parliamentary committee through which the Crown had managed affairs in the Scottish Parliament, was abolished.[7]

Now it's clear that this didn't grant sovereignty to the people. But the Scottish Parliament, an emasculated body for much of the previous century, was now free to reflect the country's proud independent traditions. For me, this is vital to an understanding of the events of 1706-7. Under the new settlement, William was expected to govern in line with the wishes of the English Parliament. But he was also expected to govern in line with the wishes of the *Scottish* Parliament. In the decade and a half leading up to 1707, the regal, security and economic issues of the two nations began seriously to diverge. The Scottish Parliament of 1703 was the most radical and restless in its history. The question is, as McLean and McMillan put it, why the "same members of the Edinburgh Parliament that successfully pressed [an] anti-English agenda voted, within three years, to pass an Act of parliamentary union that removed all legislative power to London"[8]. One might more easily have foreseen a severing of the Union of Crowns.

The historian Paul H. Scott is right, emphatically so, when he says that England was very keen on forming a Union with Scotland. But it was a sudden desire, not a long-standing wish. Several schemes had failed through lack of English interest since that proposed by James VI.

The death of the Duke of Gloucester, Queen Anne's only surviving child, in 1700, threw the Stuart succession into doubt. The resulting Act of Settlement of 1701 specifically excluded the dying Catholic James VII. He was being cosseted by France's Louis XIV at the Sun King's old palace of St Germain-en-Laye, close to Versailles. Instead, the resolutely Protestant Sophia of Hanover and her descendants were chosen to assume the British throne after Anne's death. The Scottish Parliament wasn't consulted.

After James VII's death, Louis XIV recognised his son James Frances Edward Stuart as James VIII and III. This gave succour to the Jacobites in Britain. The expansionist Louis was also keen to get his hands on the Spanish crown. That would give him control of an empire which also included Flanders and much of South America.[9] And so began the War of the Spanish Succession, ranging half a million men under Louis against the Duke of Marlborough's forces. Again, Scotland wasn't consulted. But many Scots, including Argyll, were at his side. Central to Marlborough's strategy was union between Scotland and England. He didn't want old friends of France in Scotland to give Louis a toehold from which to launch an invasion of England.

The economic situation was just as important as these developments. Climate change and crop failure meant Scotland had suffered grievous famine in the "ill years" of the late 1690s. The abortive imperial venture at Darien in Panama – which wasted a quarter of the country's liquid capital – was at least in part William's fault. He was opposed to Scotland establishing its own independent trading entrêpot. More generally, English restrictions on Scottish trade were prohibitive. Scotland was desperate to secure free trade with England. It was also keen to protect vulnerable industries.

Against this backdrop, it is easy to understand why the radical Scottish Parliament of 1703 passed acts asserting its own right to decide on the Succession, declare war and import French goods. English retaliation was rapid. The Alien Act "threatened to treat the Scots as aliens, and restrict trade in cattle, linen and coal"[10]. It was, as Tom Devine has vividly described it, "a naked piece of economic blackmail, designed to bring the Scottish parliament swiftly to the negotiating table"[11]. It worked.

The Scots failed to realise how desperate England was to secure Union. Although they were to win concessions when the Treaty passed through Parliament in 1706-7 – largely as a result of public pressure – they could have done much better when negotiating its terms in the spring and summer of 1706, particularly a more generous financial settlement.

The first mistake, infamously, was the Duke of Hamilton's. As leader of the country party opposition, Hamilton was an extraordinarily popular figure, both in and out of Parliament. He loved the adulation. But in a late night debate he betrayed his supporters. He granted to Queen Anne the right to choose the Scottish commissioners who would go to London to negotiate the terms of a Treaty of Union. Some view Hamilton as a Trojan horse – a noble plant to undermine the opposition cause. Certainly, he was keeper for Queen Anne of the Palace of Holyroodhouse, and he harboured secret hopes of becoming King of Scotland. But in truth, he was torn between a devotion to the cause of Scotland's independence and self-interest. Later, given the opportunity to lead his supporters out of Parliament and kill off the treaty, he was to blame toothache for his failing to appear.

When the Treaty was published in early October 1706, there was a public outcry in Scotland. It provided for:

an incorporating Union, which meant abolition of the ScottishParliament and significantly reduced representation at Westminster

free trade between Scotland and England although English duties were to be imposed

the Hanoverian succession

payment of an Equivalent of almost £400,000 to cover Darien losses and Scotland's share of the English national debt.

Yet the opposition was disparate. No one, apart from Fletcher of Saltoun, had articulated an alternative to incorporating union.

His federal scheme placed so many limitations on the monarchy that it failed to gain widespread support.

When Lord Belhaven, for the opposition, made his famous speech, shouting out "Good God, Is this an entire surrender?" Lord Marchmont responded, quoting Samuel, "Behold, he dreamed, but lo! when he awoke, he found it was a dream".

The granting of security to the Kirk in a separate but allied act drew away much of the opposition. Queensberry's Court Party was organised and disciplined. And Roxburghe's *squadrone volante* had become convinced of the benefits of Union.

Much is made of the £20,000 in bribes and the Equivalent in persuading members to drop their opposition. But one must remember that the venal culture was very much the *modus vivendi*. "Even the greatest offices of state were for sale: the first Earl of Manchester paid £15,000 to be made Lord Chief Justice and later paid £20,000 to be made Lord Treasurer."[12] In any case, most of the £20,000 went to Queensberry, who despite claims to the contrary did not need to be convinced of the cause. Furthermore, there was too much cohesion in the voting – ie. along parliamentary grouping lines – for bribery to have been the cause of votes shifting.

Finally, to dispel the notion that the Equivalent swayed votes, McLean and McMillan[13] show that there was no difference between the way Darien shareholders and non-Darien shareholders voted.

In conclusion, if one accepts that Scotland was at least partly a sovereign country prior to Union, one cannot logically argue that it was subject to a wholesale takeover by England. That would have been conquest. Rather, forced to choose between the disastrous and the unpalatable, Scotland opted for the latter.

"The Treaty of Union was a true treaty from which both sides gained, but both made concessions."[14] Scotland lost its Parliament but gained access to English markets. The fact that the economy failed to flourish for a further 20 years is irrelevant. The Scots didn't have a crystal ball. Scotland also preserved an independent Kirk, independent universities and an independent legal system.

As John Clerk of Penicuik, was later to put it, "What could we then do but seriously think of an Union as the only Remedy . . ."[15]

2

THE TREATY: PUBLISH AND BE DAMNED

"I had not been there long but I heard a great noise and looking saw a terrible multitude come up the High Street with a drum at the head of them and swearing and crying out all Scotland would stand together, No Union, No Union."

Daniel Defoe

3rd October 2006

Three hundred years ago today, the Scottish Parliament met at the beginning of what was to be its final session to discuss the 25 articles of the Treaty of Union of the Two Kingdoms of Scotland and England.

The articles had been drawn up by commissioners from both sides of the Border, all named – infamously, at the suggestion of James, the fourth Duke of Hamilton – by Queen Anne. The commissioners had agreed the principle of an incorporating Union, the only political solution the English negotiators would accept.

Yet until this final session the details of the treaty had been kept secret for fear, correctly as it turned out, that the Scottish public would be extremely hostile. As the author and polemicist Daniel Defoe, who had been sent to Edinburgh as an English spy, later wrote: "The people cried out, they were Scotsmen and would be Scotsmen still; they contemned the name of the Britons . . . Thus they filled the mouths of the common people, who would go about the street crying, 'no Union', and call the treaters traitors, and soon began to threaten them to their faces."

The first article stated: "That the two Kingdoms of Scotland and England, shall upon the 1st May next . . . and forever after, be United into One Kingdom by the name of Great Britain."

But the most contentious was Article 15, the Equivalent, which granted £398,085 10s, ostensibly to offset future liability towards England's national debt, but much of which was used to compensate those Scots who had invested heavily in the ill-fated Darien scheme, Scotland's folly-ridden imperial adventure in Panama which is estimated to have cost the country 25 per cent of its liquid capital assets.

This meeting of parliament was the start of a series of heated debates in the chamber and outside – and one of the most febrile episodes in Scottish history.

4th October 2006

While the last session of the old Scottish Parliament began on 3rd October, 1706, the Treaty of Union had been drafted by commissioners appointed by Queen Anne. Negotiations on its wording took place much earlier in the year, from April to July, appropriately enough in the Cockpit at Westminster.

With Scotland in financial difficulties following the Darien disaster and the famines of the last few years of the 17th century, and England desperate to prevent Scotland becoming a focal point for a French attack for a putative Catholic Stuart restoration given Queen Anne's difficulty in producing an heir, the scene was set.

The proceedings of the commissioners are among the most contested episodes in Scottish history. For some, the Scottish commissioners were all men who had previously accepted English government appointments and were therefore used to accepting English instructions, and whose self-interest lay with a union even though they knew it would be unpalatable to their fellow Scots at home. For others, the balance of power was such that incorporation of Scotland by England was inevitable, and the Scottish commissioners secured as much as they could.

Thus Paul H. Scott, the author of *The Union of 1707: why and how?*, who is very much in the former camp, quotes one of the commissioners, George Lockhart, as saying that the "English cannot be blam'd for making the best bargain they could for their own country, when they found the Scots so very complaisant, as to agree to everything that was demanded of them, managing all matters in a private club".

Historian Professor Christopher A Whatley, in his book *The Scots and the Union*, takes the opposite view. He writes: "To say that 'most' members on both sides of the table in the Cockpit . . . considered their own future rather than that of the two kingdoms, is an assertion based on the predisposition of an individual historian rather than a statement of fact derived from the body of evidence that would be required to substantiate it."

The draft Treaty was approved on 16th July and signed and sealed six days later, before being presented to Queen Anne on 23rd July.

The alternative to the Treaty of Union would almost certainly have been an invasion of Scotland by a much more powerful England. Lord Keeper William Cooper said: "The great and main consequence of the Treaty . . . was the continuation of peace and tranquility . . . instead of the bloodshed and distraction which would probably follow upon the fatal division of it."

5th October 2006

Many extraordinary characters were involved in the events that led to the Act of Union of 1707, but none perhaps more so than James, fourth Duke of Hamilton.

In the portrait of him by Sir Godfrey Kneller, in which he is resplendently, if incongruously, dressed in a suit of body armour and an extravagantly looping King Charles wig, he looks away from the viewer in a shifty fashion out of the side of his eyes. It is a painting that got the measure of the man.

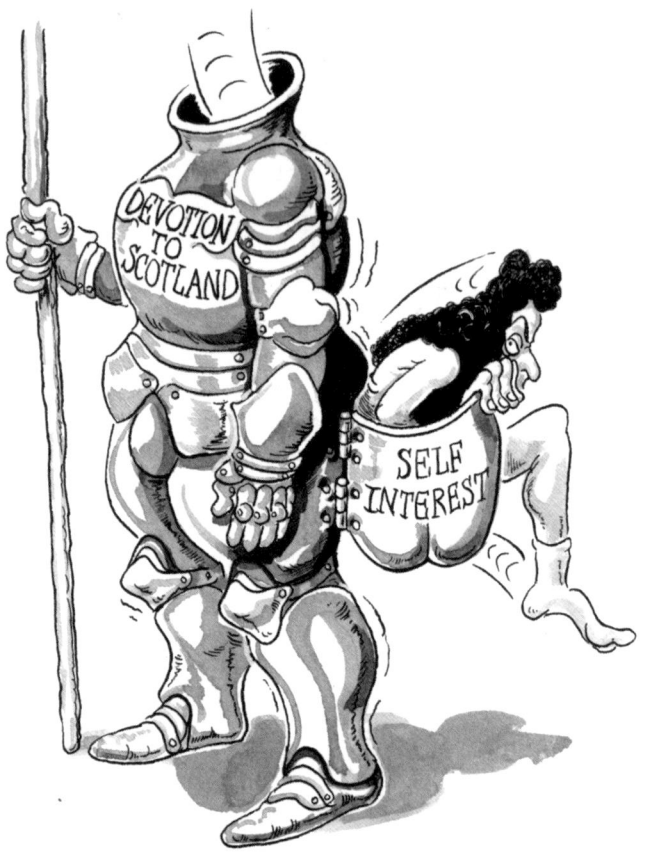

James was a member of what was and still remains a
distinguished Scottish political dynasty. He was the leader of the
Country party, which ostensibly represented Scotland's national
interest in opposition to the English-government supporting Court
party led by the Duke of Queensberry, who had been personally
appointed to the Scottish Parliament by the monarch.

However, Hamilton had inherited an estate in England through
marriage. Thus, while emotionally in touch with the anti-Unionist

mood of the majority of Scots, he was rationally in favour of uniting Scotland and England; not least did he favour a government position.

Hamilton was to be accused of betrayal when, on 1st September, 1705, at the end of a long day's parliamentary debate on whether a group of commissioners should be nominated to discuss a possible union, he proposed that the Scottish commissioners be appointed by Queen Anne. It wasn't to be the last time that he abandoned the cause of the Country party yet, oddly, he was to remain popular both among politicians and the crowds in Edinburgh.

The historian GM Trevelyan wrote of Hamilton's act in relation to the Union that it was "the instrument under Heaven of its almost miraculous passage". His own mother said: "I am so ashamed on his behalfe that I know neither what to say or how to look."

Despite Jacobite sympathies (he was descended from the Stuarts), he was expedient in seeking good relations with Queen Anne, declaring his love for her on the day of the final vote on the Union in parliament. When the vote in favour was announced, Hamilton cried: "No."

Queen Anne gave him a British peerage in 1710, the Dukedom of Brandon, and two years later he became Ambassador to France. Soon after, he died in a duel in London.

6th October 2006

While the Duke of Hamilton was the leader of the "opposition", the leader of the Court party was the Duke of Queensberry, the man who would eventually succeed in creating the Union.

In his book *The Union: England, Scotland and the Treaty of 1707*, the historian Michael Fry describes Queensberry as "ruthless and covetous, yet friendly and funny; a deep streak of dishonesty helped him to plot devious paths to distant goals because he could see through his fellows' lesser concerns".

Queensberry had been appointed Lord High Commissioner of the Scottish Parliament for a spell by King William, whose trust in him was strong. On his deathbed, William had advocated Union; after his death Queen Anne followed suit – and reappointed

Queensberry as her man in Scotland. Along with the Earls of Seafield, Mar, Loudoun and Glasgow, he was later generally accepted to have taken a bribe from the Queen to ensure she got her way. Some £20,000 was made available in the form of a loan, which was to be repaid through the civil list, and Queensberry secured most of this money – £12,300. Part of this fund was for his previous services. In his memoirs George Lockhart of Carnwath, one of the few Scottish commissioners who was not a friend of Queensberry, alleged that the Lord High Commissioner had been paid twice.

When the terms of the Treaty of Union were revealed early in October 1706 there was uproar among the public in Edinburgh and beyond. Queensberry became the focus of much of this anger. When his coach went through the city it was pelted with stones and excrement from the streets.

Yet he imposed enough discipline on the Court party to push through the Act, and on 25th March, 1707, stated: "I am persuaded that we and our posterity will reap the benefit of the Union of the two kingdoms, and I doubt not, that as this Parliament has had the honour to conclude it, you will in your several stations recommend to the people of the nation a grateful sense of Her Majesty's goodness and great care for the welfare of her subjects in bringing this important affair to perfection, and that you will promote an universal desire in this kingdom to become one in hearts and affection, as we are inseparably joined in interest with our neighbour nation."

Depending on your point of view, it was either ironic or a deliberate act of historical point-scoring by Donald Dewar that the new Scottish Parliament building at Holyrood incorporated Queensberry House, which the duke had built in 1695.

9th October 2006

While Hamilton and Queensberry were among the great Scottish characters of the era that led to Union, the best remembered Englishman of the whole debacle is undoubtedly Daniel Defoe, even if his fame derives in large part from his remarkable works of literature, including *Robinson Crusoe*.

Defoe was appointed by Robert Harley as a spy for the English to watch over the final session of the Scottish Parliament, which began in October 1706.

Harley, the scheming English secretary of state under Queen Anne, sent Defoe north with a brief to give the impression he was there on his own business. He was, however, to send word at least once a week to two false addresses on "the true state of how you find things". And he was also to act as a propagandist for the Union: "You must show them this is such an opportunity that being once lost or neglected is not again to be recovered."

In *The Union*, Michael Fry notes of Harley and Defoe: "In tandem they made a good controller and agent, each after his own way considerate of human nature while harbouring no illusions about it."

Defoe replaced William Paterson, a founder of the Bank of England, but also one of the leaders of the ill-fated Darien scheme in Panama, which put paid to Scotland's colonial ambitions. Paterson was judged unsuccessful because, in the face of obvious public opposition, he kept indicating that Union was a done deal.

Defoe informed Harley that although the Union had been agreed by the commissioners, its passage in Edinburgh was not guaranteed, particularly because of the opposition of the Presbyterian Church of Scotland. He reported how, while going about Edinburgh, as he ascended a stair a group of Scots said: "There is one of the English dogs."

The following night, on the street, the "rabble" was out again: "I had not been there long but I heard a great noise and looking saw a terrible multitude come up the High Street with a drum at the head of them and swearing and crying out all Scotland would stand together, No Union, No Union."

In 1709, Defoe would write *A History of the Union*, arguing that Union was the only way for the Scots to become rich and happy and avoid "popery, French usurpations and spurious succession". In other words, as the Jacobite cause gathered strength, Scotland could maintain its mainly Presbyterian religious identity, avoid manipulation by Louis XIV and accept the chosen English succession of the House of Hanover.

10th October 2006

When the terms of the Treaty of Union became publicly known 300 years ago this month, there was an outcry among the general population of Scots, the vast majority of whom were opposed to incorporation with England. Anti-Union songs and poems, many printed, others handwritten or passed on verbally, poked fun at pro-Union politicians.

Rioting broke out, first in Edinburgh, then, in November, in Glasgow. In the capital, one witness described the "disorderly and insolent convocations, and gathering of commons, filling the streets with clamour and confusion, and insulting not only peaceable persons but also some of the members of our high and honourable court of parliament, presuming to threaten and invade them in their very dwelling-houses". The town guard, made up of ex-soldiers, was hopeless, and when the mob tried to break into Parliament House, the government called for troops garrisoned at Edinburgh Castle.

William Johnston, the Marquis of Annandale, opposed this deployment from parliament's benches, saying: "Shall we, who live in a free kingdom, put up with this barbarous restriction even before we have agreed to join our kingdom to another? This Union spells death to our nation's liberty, but not until it is passed into law should we be ringing our parliament with troops."

Fears for their own safety meant that, realistically, all the members of parliament could do was condemn the rioters; predictably, with no-one able to stop them, trouble continued.

The rioting was often triggered by the appearance of the Duke of Hamilton on the Royal Mile between parliament and Holyrood. Insults and ordure often rained down on the chair of Queensberry, the man who finally secured the Union for Queen Anne. Daniel Defoe told his spymasters in London that Queensberry continued to be threatened with assassination.

Later, as these concerns spread through the English government at Westminster, English troops were mustered and stationed on the Scottish Border. Yet, although he came close to doing so, in the event Queensberry had no need to call on them to intervene.

But opposition to the Treaty was not confined to the "rabble". Shortly after publication, the Kirk, through the Commission of the General Assembly, indicated its opposition: after all, there was no mention in the Treaty of the Kirk, and a plan to place Scots in the House of Lords along with 26 bishops was "a violation of the Covenant" that had dispensed with Episcopalian Church government north of the Border.

11th October 2006

Despite the fact that English ministers promised its nature and activities would remain unaltered by Union with England, the stiffest opposition to the Treaty came from the Church of Scotland.

In part, the suspicions of Presbyterian Scots can be explained by living memory of major developments in the country's tortuous religious history. After all, in 1706 it was less than 70 years since the National Covenant was signed by huge numbers of Scots in protest at Charles I's secretly developed Prayer Book and other innovations designed to jazz up "plain" Church of Scotland services. This followed the Bishops' Wars.

The inaptly named "Glorious Revolution" of 1688-89, in which the Catholic King James VII and II was deposed and replaced by the staunchly Protestant William of Orange, was even fresher in the memory. (The Jacobites, named thus after Jacobus, the Latin for James, would also oppose the Union, principally because it would secure the Protestant Hanoverian succession on the death of Queen Anne).

In 1690, the Kirk was re-established in law as Scotland's national church; however, in contrast to the practice in the Church of England, of which the monarch was the titular head, the King was made a member of the Kirk only.

Yet, the jitters remained strongly in evidence, as Professor Christopher Whatley states in his book *The Scots and the Union*: "Church of Scotland ministers and elders felt no more secure in practice than they had on the late king's death [King William died in 1702], and in the spring launched another offensive . . . against

Episcopalian preachers . . . to counter the growing strength of popery."

Even if the Kirk was to remain untouched, many ministers feared for Scots Presbyterians who moved south – technically, they would be treated as dissenters by the Church of England, despite being a member of an established church. And might not a new British Parliament introduce a Toleration Act allowing Episcopalians to practice freely? (This fear was indeed to be borne out in 1712.)

Of most immediate concern to Kirk members in 1706, however, was that the Treaty made no mention of their institution. Shortly after the terms were announced, the Commission of the General Assembly declared it unacceptable. Members feared that incorporation by the English state would imperil the very existence of the Kirk.

As Queensberry's aide, the Earl of Mar, wrote to English Secretary of State Lord Godolphin: "The humour in the country against the treaty or Union is much increased of late . . . the ministers preaching up the danger of the Kirk is a principal cause of it."

3

LET BATTLE COMMENCE

"It was a long night for everyone, but especially for those who favoured union: no one was safe in his own home."

John Clerk of Penicuik

12th October 2006

It was 300 years today that the Scottish Parliament began considering the Treaty of Union. Lord Queensberry's aide, the Earl of Mar, opened proceedings by proposing that the 25 articles be considered one by one.

Whereas in previous sessions of parliament, Queensberry, as Lord High Commissioner, had failed to maintain discipline in the Court party, this time he was able to impose his will.

But arguably much more significant was the failure of the opposition to unify, enabling Queensberry to push through the terms of the treaty against the wishes of the majority of the Scottish public.

As already noted, much of the opposition came from Scots Presbyterians concerned about the future independence of their institution – both from the State and episcopalianism.

Indeed, Walter Stewart of Pardovan, the member for Linlithgow and described by Michael Fry as a "militant Presbyterian", demanded – unsuccessfully – that the security of the Kirk be guaranteed before a single article was discussed.

Outside parliament, more radical Kirk figures suggested that violence might be necessary to block the Union.

Yet moderates in the Kirk were deeply concerned about the prospect of the mob running wild – as much for what it could portend as for being inherently wrong. They feared the English would invade to crush opposition or – and for some this was worse – open the way to the Jacobites and restoration of the Catholic Stewart monarchy. The learned Rev Robert Wodrow, for a time Glasgow University's librarian and then minister in the Parish of Eastwood, described violence as "the best handle the Jacobites ever had". The arrival of the Pretender wearing a "mask of protestantism" would be disastrous for the Kirk.

In parliament, the Duke of Hamilton described the issue of union as an "affair of the greatest concern and import" which mattered more than "any thing [that] ever was before this house". Such was its historical import, he suggested, that it would be wise to place before the house the records of previous negotiations over possible unions, to which Queensberry agreed.

Procedural wranglings like this meant it was not until 15th October that members got round to resolving to move on to a first reading of the Treaty. Then the fireworks began.

13th October 2006

Scottish laird George Lockhart of Carnwath, a Jacobite, was the only commissioner appointed by Queen Anne who opposed the Treaty. In his memoirs, he gave a frank and honest account of how Scotland and England became joined in Union. Between 12th and 15th October, 1706, the Scottish Parliament resolved to proceed to consider the articles of the Treaty one by one. Lockhart wrote:

On the fifteenth the Court [party] moved that . . . the house should proceed to the consideration of the articles of union. There were many opposed to this as too hasty a procedure in so momentous an affair, and craved liberty . . . to consider and advise with their constituents [on the articles]. From whence arose a hot debate, whether or not the Parliament, without particular instructions from their constituents, could alter the constitution of the government. The court [said it could] since the members had ample commissions to do all things for the good of the country, and that one of the reasons assigned in the proclamation for summoning this Parliament was to consider on ways and means to unite the two kingdoms.

To which it was replyed . . . that everybody knew the nation had nothing of the Union in their view at the time this Parliament was chosen. Besides, [the election, in 1703] was so long ago that it was not strange the barons, freeholders and burghs expected their representatives should advise with them. And since they were not allowed to have a new election, that thus their sense of this weighty affair might be known in Parliament, that it would tend much more to the honour of the commissioners of the Treaty if it was approved of in a Parliament called for that purpose, or by members who had received the fresh instructions and opinions of the nation, than by a Parliament which had continued so long, and thereby so many of its members corrupted by bribes, pensions, places and preferments . . . At length a vote was stated in these words, 'Proceed to consider the articles of the treaty or delay?' But it carried in the affirmative by a plurality of sixty-four voices, and all that the Country party could obtain was that the house should not proceed to vote and approve any of the articles until they were all once read and discoursed on by the members . . . The Country party particularly the Dukes of Hamilton and Athol, the Marquis of Annandale, the Lords Belhaven and Balmerino [and] Mr Fletcher of Salton [sic] . . . took a great deal of pains to expose the unreasonableness of the several articles . . . but the Courtiers very seldom made any reply, having resolved to trust to their number of led-horses and not to trouble themselves with reasoning.

18th October 2006

Amid the ferment over proposals for union, the Kirk set aside 18th October, 1706, as a day of national prayer; it was followed by another day of prayer and fasting on 22 October.

John Clerk of Penicuik, who became the Unionists' Lockhart with a pro-incorporation memoir, noted:

> While parliament and the city were in turmoil, the Commission of the General Assembly of the Church of Scotland, then sitting, began to consider how best in this emergency to look after their own interests and those of the church committed to their charge ... They decided by a large majority to start by instituting a period of prayer and fasting, to be observed publicly as well as in private, asking God to guide the deliberations of parliament and people for the good of the church and the nation. Their right to do this was later questioned, since customarily prayer and fasting could only be ordered by parliament or the monarch. Many, however, claimed this jurisdiction for the church by Divine Right.
>
> Attempts to endorse these religious proposals were made by several members of parliament, chiefly opponents of union who were far from being wholeheartedly concerned to uphold the Church's authority. They jumped eagerly at the chance of espousing the fast, primarily in the hope of winning ministers and people to their side. But most members were outraged by this jesting with religion. 'In the case of plague,' some said, 'or war, or famine, it is right for us to fast and to pray to God sincerely to prevent or remove such calamities. But such is not the case now. The effect of this will be to aggravate anger and conflict, to excite the populace to violence and disorder by making them afraid of some impending catastrophe.'
>
> History shows us that fasts have very often been instituted for trivial, indeed thoroughly discreditable reasons, enabling ambitious or revolutionary leaders to win popular favour and get away with their crimes.
>
> Prayer and fasting has been a common trick of unscrupulous politicians . . . 'If prayers are to be offered, let us ask that God will favour this long-sought union of the British kingdoms and bless us by granting our wishes.' But the ministers fought pretty resolutely

in the matter of prayer and fasting, for the spirit of faction had got into them too.

They finally decided to send a letter exhorting ministers to institute fasts in their separate congregations and parishes. These were as solemnly observed as those normally ordained by parliament or the monarch, which was all the more gratifying to the clerics because they saw it as a mark of that absolute authority vested in the Church which they had long sought and claimed.

19th October 2006

The Kirk's opposition to the Treaty of Union was by no means unique in civil society; and as the Scottish Parliament began to debate its terms, unrest became apparent not only in Edinburgh but across the country.

In his Memoirs, Lockhart of Carnwath captures the strength of feeling very well:

> If we now leave the town [Edinburgh] and make a tour through the country, though the badness of the season prevented their coming together and proceeding to acts of violence, yet there we shall find the same, if not a greater, aversion to the Union, which amongst other things appears from the addresses that were presented during this session of Parliament from several shires, stewartries, burghs, towns and parishes situated in all corners of the land, Whig and Tory, Presbyterian and episcopal, south and north, all agreeing against the Union.
>
> I know very well . . . that vile monster and wretch Daniel Defoe, and other mercenary tools and trumpeters of rebellion, have often asserted that these addresses and other instances of the nation's aversion to the Union, proceeded from the false glosses and underhand dealings of those that opposed it in Parliament, whereby the meaner sort were imposed upon and deluded into those jealousies and measures. I shall not deny but perhaps this measure had its first original, as they report. But it is absolutely false to say that any sinister means were used to bring in subscribers. The contrary is notoriously known, for the people flocked together to sign them and expressed their resentments with the greatest indignation. Neither was it from a mobbish humourish fit that this proceeded, for the barons and

freeholders, being denied the liberty of giving instructions to their representatives, entered into this measure as the most proper to signify their inclinations to them, and it is not to be expressed what a value, I may say veneration, the commons shewed for the soveraignty, which they expressed by exclaiming against the taking away the crown and laws of the land.

20th October 2006

Opposition to the Union that was apparent in different parts of the country reached parliament on 20th October, 1706, when the mob gathered baying for blood. John Clerk of Penicuik described this as "a memorable day which seemed likely to put an end not only to discussion of any form of union for all time to come but also to the authority of parliament and the lives of the delegates who had treated with the English". He went on:

For when debate had continued until nightfall, and darkness had emboldened those lurking outside, the Commissioner [Queensberry] was surrounded as he unsuspectingly left the house to go home. He was shouted at, almost knocked down by stones, and would surely have been killed if his guards had not hurried him off to the palace . . . What the conspiracy lacked above all was a leader . . . Though many had secretly fomented insurrection, no one was bold enough to lead it openly. The Duke of Hamilton led the anti-union faction in parliament, and the rioters called on him to lead them too; his popularity was such that he would deny them nothing. As he left Parliament Hall they greeted him as their chief and begged him to take charge of the kingdom in its hour of peril. Promising to do whatever he told them, they accompanied him to the home of his brother-in-law, the Duke of Atholl . . . While the mob stood waiting for orders outside . . . their anger boiled over in a dastardly attack on the Lord Provost of Edinburgh, Patrick Johnston, who lived in the vicinity. Johnston . . . was a defenceless, harmless man, well-deserving in all other respects. But the crowd decided to do away with him. They rushed straight to his house and set about trying to break down the door with beams and any instruments they could lay their hands on. Alarmed by the noise, his wife ran to the window in desperation; her loud cries for help roused the city guard who came to the rescue. Dispersing as best they could, six of the trouble-makers were taken and imprisoned. Thus the provost [and his] family was saved, but the rising was by no means put down.

23th October 2006

Patrick Johnston, the Lord Provost of Edinburgh, was saved from the mob, but the crowd continued [to agitate]. John Clerk of Penicuik takes up the story again:

It was a long night for everyone, but especially for those who favoured union: no one was safe in his own home.

Among the [rabble's] projects . . . was one to seize the lower gate of the city and prevent the Queen's militia from coming to the aid of the guard. In this way they thought to bring the unionist majority in parliament under their control. But by the grace of God and the Destiny of Britain, help came in time to prevent these disasters.

The Commissioner got wind of the plan. He reckoned that it was safer to infringe some of the city's laws and privileges than to allow it to be taken over by the frenzy of criminals. Delay on his part would encourage the mob; a long-smouldering fire would erupt into a great conflagration. He recalled that outbreaks of civil war almost always stemmed from the negligence and sloth of magistrates. They were easily prevented, but once blood had been shed soon got out of control, so that harsher measures had to be applied. So, after obtaining the approval of some members of the Town Council, the Commissioner instructed the militia to restore order in the city and keep watch over the safety of parliament and the populace.

As well as bringing peace, the army's entry into the city put a brake on similar disturbances in future. The plotters began to recognise the gravity of their actions, and that slighting the Queen's majesty and the authority of her Commissioner and parliament would not go unpunished.

. . . The Commissioner's action which brought peace to the city was maliciously criticised, and the leave given to the army to enter the gates was loudly and bitterly condemned.

Some said it was unthinkable for a free parliament in a free kingdom to be surrounded by troops. Parliament seemed under attack, as though members were being forced to alter their votes to suit a handful of courtiers ... But the real cause of anger soon became clear: the opposition's hope of provoking riots and forcing the dissolution of parliament had been frustrated. Trusting in the mildness of a woman's rule . . . they had thought they could get away with anything.

Afterwards, all they could do was to try to win over the militia to their side, which they did with all manner of flattering speeches and bribes, appealing to them to abandon the cause of union and go against the Queen's wishes.

24th October 2006

The writer Daniel Defoe was employed as a spy by the English Tory government official Robert Harley and was sent to Scotland to report back on the proceedings of the Scottish Parliament as it debated the Treaty of Union. He wrote his first letter 300 years ago today, on 24th October:

I am sorry to tell you here is a most confused scene of affaires, and the Ministry have a very difficult course to steer ... We have two mobs .. and expect a third and of these the following is a short account.

The first was in the [Kirk General] Assembly or Commission of Assembly where very strange things were talk'd of and in a strange manner and I confess such as has put me much out of love with ecclesiastic parliamts ... I confess they contribute too much to the generall aversion which here is to the Union, at the same time they acknowledge they are uneasy in their present establishment – I work incessantly with them ... They mean well but are blinded in their politicks and obstinate in opinion.

But we had the last two nights a worse mob than this and that was in the street, and certainly a Scots rabble is the worst of its kind. The first night they onely threatned hard and follow'd their patron [the Duke of] Hamilton's chair with huzzas from the parliament House quite thro' the city – they came up again hallowing in the dark, threw some stones at the guard, broke a few windows and the like, and so it ended.

I was warn'd that night that I should take care of my self and not appear in the street which indeed for the last five dayes I have done . . . However, I went up the street in a friends coach in the evening and some of the mob not then got together were heard to say when I went into a house, there was one of the English dogs &c.

I casually stayd at the house I went then till dark and thinking to return to my lodging, found the wholl city in a most dreadfull uproar and the high street full of the rabble.

Duke Hamilton came from the house in his chair as usual and instead of going down the city to his lodgings went up the High street it was said to visit the [Duke] of Athol.

This whether design'd by the [Duke of Hamilton] as most think or no, but if not was exactly calculated to begin the tumult – for the mob in a vast crow'd attending him thither waited at the door – and as people did not come there to be idle, the Duke could have done nothing more directly to the point out their bussiness . . .

[Later] I heard a great noise and looking out saw a terrible multitude come up the High street with a drum at the head of them shouting and swearing and crying out all Scotland would stand together, No Union, No Union, English dogs, and the like.

25th October 2006

In his second letter to Harley, the English spy Daniel Defoe wrote:

I have not faild since I came hither to give you a constant and faithfull account of every thing which occurs on this stage of confusion. I am every day a member of the generall assembly and I confess I make a very odd figure here, for all day the commission sits, and night and morning I have a Revrend Committee . . .

In my last you had an account of two mobs, in perticular church and street, but as you were put in expectation of a third mob there, I purposely refer'd it to this post to let you know that this particular sort is expected within the house it self.

There is an entire harmony in this country consisting in universall discords. The church men in perticular are goeing mad. The parsons are out of their wits and those who at first were brought over, and pardon me were some of them my converts, their country brethren being now come in are all come back and to be brought over by no perswasion.

The mob you have heard of are affrighted with the loss of the Scots crown – and the parsons malitiously humour it, and a country parson who preach't yesterday at the high Kirk before the Commissonr took this text, Behold I Come Quickly. Hold fast that which thou hast; let no man take thy Crown. He pretended not to mean an earthly crown but made his wholl sermon a bald allegory against the Union. I confess I had patience to hear him but to an exceeding mortification.

The third mob is expected in the house where tis said when the party see the articles put to the vote, if they can not carry their part, they will protest, take instruments as they call it here and leav the house, and then they pretend to say the nation will take arms and the high lands are to be brought in – and indeed if this should run so far I fear the church will joyn the worst of their enemies against the Union.

They are now a goeing to fast all over the kingdome and therin to give the ministers occasion to pray and preach against it, and soon as that is done tumultuous addresses are preparing in severall parts of the country.

And thus you see sir what a nation you have to do with here. I am as diligent, with caution not to be suspected, as possible, I have not the success I hop't for but I continue to push on and think I do no harm.

I have printed one essay which I transmitted the last post. I have the second in the press, which if it does equall service with the first I shall not so much grutch the expence.

... I beseech you Sir to concern your self in the case that I may not be ruind while I am at this distance, my secret enemies being very vigilant and furious.

4

THE CRACKDOWN

"Shall we, who live in a free kingdom, put up with this barbarous restriction even before we have agreed to join our kingdom to another?"

Marquis of Annandale

26th October 2006

Following the violence meted out by the Edinburgh mob, as described by the English spy Daniel Defoe, Queen Anne issued a proclamation against "tumults and rabbles", which was read and then posted across the city. It gives a valuable insight into the mood of the times – and the harsh nature of justice that would often be meted out.

In co-opting "regents and masters" at Edinburgh University to look out for signs of restiveness among their students, it raises a chilling parallel with our current government's desire for academics to 'spy' on Muslim students. The proclamation stated:

> [T]he raising of tumults [is] a most dangerous, pernicious and unboundable practice, contrary to the very being and foundation of government, and destructive of the chief ends thereof, the safety and security of mens living and fortunes . . .

There happened within these few days, and particularly on the Twenty Third . . . and near to the Parliament House, and in the Parliament Close, even [at] the time of sitting, and at the rising of the High and Honourable Court of Parliament, when our High Commissioner was present among them, most disorderly and insolent convocation, and gathering of commons, filling the streets with clamour and confusion, and insulting not only peacable persons, but also some of the members of our said High and Honourable Court of Parliament, presuming to threaten and invade them in their dwelling houses, by a most villainous and outrageous mobb, which all persons of justice, honour and reason ought to detest, and endeavour to suppress, and prevent, in the severest and strictest manner.

Therefore we in the just resentment of such high indignities, have thought fit, with the advice of our Lords of the Privy Council, to ordain the magistrates of Edinburgh to . . . make strict inquiries and search, and to cause apprehend all the authors, abetters, accessaries, or affiliates of the aforesaid convocations, mobbs and tumults to the effect that they may be brought to condign punishment . . .

[We] also call [on] the Regents and Masters of the College of Edinburgh, and enjoyn them strictly, that for hereafter they keep their scholars in good order, and be careful of their quiet and peaceable behaviour. And we ordain all the inhabitants of the said Burgh, readily to assist and concur with the magistrates, for repressing and punishing all tumults . . .

[In the event of a tumult we require] all and sundry to withdraw and retire to their respective houses, shops and imployments . . . Whoever shall be found therefore disobedient, and to confine upon the streets, may be attacked and seized by the town guard.

27th October 2006

After Queen Anne's proclamation against "tumults and rabbles", which informed troublemakers that they might be seized by the town guard – as described in the previous article – the Scottish Parliament passed a motion charging the Privy Council with ensuring the safety of the realm, ie keeping a lid on trouble.

But the parliament agreed to keep the army outside the city, thanks to this powerful speech by the Marquis of Annandale in defence of Edinburgh's historic charters which expressly outlawed the barracking troops inside the city walls:

Shall we, who live in a free kingdom, put up with this barbarous restriction even before we have agreed to join our kingdom to another? This union spells death to our nation's liberty, but not until it is passed into law should we be ringing our parliament with troops. See what has become of the freedom of the estates of the realm of Scotland!

Should their representatives sit mute? Should their mouths be sealed by a soldier's sword? We have all heard the story of the dumb man who thought to kill his father until love for his father taught him to cry out. Let that example teach us not to sit here in silence while our fatherland is destroyed. But in this free kingdom our tongues must be bridled by the army! What use are these soldiers who stand with drawn swords at the doors of this venerable building? Are we not safe enough within the walls of this city, long famous for its loyalty to this and all earlier parliaments? Are we not safe enough relying on our fellow citizens, whose oldest instinct has always been to guard the well-being, peace and prosperity of the kingdom? Let guilty men fear, let traitors tremble, and honour be to those who protect our freedom and our rights.

We within these walls have nothing to fear. They call us the fathers of our fatherland, and rightly; so let us care for our fatherland and serve its interests before our own, its needs before our private advantage. If any think otherwise – but I accuse none, I hope none can be so shameless – let them come to their senses; and since the fortune of Scotland has given us this chance, let us seize it in a manner worthy of our ancestors, worthy of the name of Scotland. The soldiers should go; they should go fight our enemies and win glory abroad; but if they stay here, let them act for the good of the people who provide their daily rations.

They are here, some say, to keep peace in the city. Not so! Rather to strike fear into faint hearts and restrict our freedom of expression. Free-born men must be free to debate the state of their country. And if there is to be a treaty, it will not be valid unless entered into by free peoples, acting not under duress or in fear or for promised rewards but with national interests at heart.

30th October 2006

After all the ferment in Scotland during the month of October, Parliament finally got down to considering in detail the articles of the Treaty of Union on 1st November, 1706. George Lockhart of Carnwath observed how, after abortive delaying tactics by the Country party, it was agreed that a vote in favour of the first article on the principle of union would not be binding should other articles be rejected:

> [A] motion was made that the house should proceed to the further and more particular consideration of the articles. Against which a delay was proposed by the Country party till once the sentiments of the English Parliament were known, they having once before rejected the terms of union which the commissioners of both kingdoms had agreed to and the Scots Parliament approved, and till the members had consulted their constituents, which was urged as more necessary now than formerly when the motion was made since several shires and boroughs had already addressed, and many more were preparing to address, and did shew an utter aversion to the Union.
>
> But, this delay being refused, the next resource to postpone the ratification of any of the articles was to begin at the security of the church. But that not doing either, the last of all was to urge the unreasonableness of agreeing to a Union of the two kingdoms till once they had gone through and found that the terms thereof were for the interest of this kingdom, of which once being perswaded, all the rest would go glibly down. Besides, if they should in the first place agree to the Union of the two kingdoms, subverting the monarchy and sinking the parliament . . . who knew but the royal assent might be given thereto and the Parliament adjourned, and so the nation be united upon no terms, or at best upon such as England of themselves should condescend to give us afterwards, which was compared to a young maid's yielding upon a promise of marriage, which was seldom performed.
>
> There being so much reason in the motion, the Courtiers knew not how to get over it, and the House generally inclined to it by taking the terms of the Union previously into consideration before they approved of the Union itself. But the Lord Register found a

back door whereby to make their retreat by presenting a resolve in these terms:

That it be agreed that the house in the first place proceed to take the first article of the treaty into consideration, with this proviso: that if all the other articles be not adjusted by the Parliament, then the agreeing to and approving of the first article shall be of no effect.

Which, after a long debate being put to the vote, was approved.

31st October 2006

As Parliament considered the treaty of union, the English spy Daniel Defoe wrote to his master, Harley:

Since my last the face of affaires I hope are a little mended and after a very long and warm debate on Fryday whether they should proceed on the Union or go first on the security of the Church, it was past proceed.

On Saturday they sat till near 8 at night and the speeches on both sides were long and warm. [The Duke of] Hamilton rav'd, Fletcher of Saltoun, and the Earle of Belhaven, made long speeches, the latter of which will be printed – the clamour without was so great that a rabble was feared tho' the guards are numerous and were drawn out in readyness.

Addresses are delivred in from severall places and more prepareing ... The addresses are found in the cant of the old times, deploring the misery of Scotland for want of a further reformation and the security of the Church and the Lords covenanter people, but when the names come to be examin'd they are all sign'd by known Jacobites and Episcopall men.

There has been a farther expectation of a mob and some practices have been used to infect the souldiers, but the [Earl] of Leven call'd the guards together to day and made a speech to them. They had been posesst with a notion that they should be sent to the West Indees as soon as the Union was over. My Ld Leven I hope has reestablisht them, and the proceeding since is more favourable.

Last night the grand question was put whether the first article – or in short the Union it self should be approved or not and carryed in the affirmativ which being on King Williams birthday is to me very remarkable and encouraging.

I had to day the honour to be sent for by the [Lords] committee for examining the Equivalents and to assure them in the calculating the draw back on the salt, the proportion of the excise and some addenda about trade [the Equivalents were designed to recompense Scotland for the immediate financial cost of Union while the drawbacks were refunds of customs duties that Scotland would have to give up as part of the Union].

They profess themselves oblig'd to me more than I merit and at their next committee I am desir'd to dine with them. I am lookt on as a English man that designs to settle here and I think am perfectly unsuspected and hope on that foot I do some service onely I spend you a great deal of money at which I am concern'd but see no remedy if I will go thro' with the work.

I have now great hopes of it thro' to day the assembly men make a great stir; in short the Kirk are au wood [all mad], pardon the Scotticisme.

5

DOWN TO BUSINESS

"Good God! What, is this an entire surrender!"

Lord Belhaven

1st November 2006

By the beginning of November, parliament was finally in a position to begin debating the Treaty of Union, leading to some of the most famous speeches in Scottish history, particularly that of Lord Belhaven.

In his History of the Union, Sir John Clerk of Penicuik, who was there, gives us a flavour of the arguments made in the opposition speeches:

> For many ages past, our estates have met and debated with the single goal of leaving Scotland in a better state than they found it. Why then is our single aim now to surrender disgracefully everything cherished by our ancestors and all free men, spurning and ignoring the wishes of those who put the kingdom in our care? Union is a great and hazardous matter; it is equally a great and unprecedented crime to broach fundamental change in our constitution without consulting the people. We have no jurisdiction or authority to do

so. Our authorisation is to promote Scotland, not to destroy it; to defend and augment our liberties, not throw them away ... We are now voluntarily to accept the yoke that England has threatened us with for centuries. Our liberty, that dear Scottish liberty born in blood and sweat, gloriously maintained by our fathers for our benefit, must perish in an instant. Our church, dignified and made famous by the blood of martyrs, must be utterly destroyed, shipwrecked in an ocean of Anglican ritual on the rocks of priesthood and vanity. Our towns and cities must be left defenceless and betrayed to our English rivals, their ruins an example to posterity of a nation shamefully betrayed and despoiled of its honour and dignity. We have nothing to look forward to but utter devastation, famine and poverty, and, worst of all, perpetual servitude to cruel overlords. Remember your ancestors ... for who, at the mention of their veritable names, would not take heart to be worthy of them? Call to mind the brave deeds of the Bruces, the Douglases, and such, and you will burn with the same patriotic flame and not be idle spectators of calamities to come. But they say the English offer us trading opportunities, privileges, wealth. As for trade, the whole world is open to our merchants as to other brave men, and prosperity comes through enterprise and daring. What are those English privileges we want so badly? And if their wealth is the attraction, let us not earn it as the reward of this wicked betrayal. Our country commends to us the lives of its citizens, the dignity of its parliament, the majesty of its throne, the sanctity of its church, and the care of its rights and privileges and commerce, for today's decision affects the fate of this assembly, our sovereignty and freedom, all that is dearest to us, the welfare of our people and their children.

2nd November 2006

The most famous of the many fine speeches made by members of the parliament on the Union is undoubtedly that of the nationalist, Lord Belhaven, on this day in 1706. Here are some highlights:

When I consider the affair of a Union betwixt the two nations ... I find my mind crouded with variety of melancholy thoughts ...

I think I see a free and independent kingdom delivering up that which all the world hath been fighting for since the days of Nimrod; yea, that for which most of all the empires, kingdoms, states, principalities, and dukedoms of Europe are at this time engaged in the most bloody and cruel wars that ever were, to wit, a power to manage their own affairs by themselves . . .

I think I see a national Church, founded upon a rock, secured by a Claim of Right, heged and fenced about, by the strictest and most pointed legal sanction that sovereignty could contrive, voluntarily descending into a plain, upon an equal level with Jews, Papists, Socinians, Arminians, Anahaptists . . .

I think I see the present peers of Scotland, whose noble ancestors conquered provinces, over-run countries, reduced and subjected towns and fortified places, exacted tribute through the greatest part of England, now walking in the court of requests like so many English attorneys . . .

I think I see the Royal state of burghs walking their desolate streets, hanging down their heads under disappointmen, wormed out of all their old trade, uncertain what hand to turn to, necessitate to become 'prentices to their unkind neighbours; and yet after all, finding their trade so fortified by companies, and secured by prescriptions, that they despair of any success therein . . .

I think I see the honest industrious tradesman loaded with new taxes and impositions . . . drinking water in place of ale, eating his saltless pottage

. . . In short, I think I see the laborious ploughman, with his corn spoiling upon his hands, for want of sale, cursing the day of his birth, dreading the expence of his burial, and uncertain whether to marry or do worse

But above all, my Lord, I think I see our ancient Mother Caledonia, like Caesar, sitting in the midst of our Senate, ruefully looking round about her, covering herself with her royal garment, attending the fatal blow, and breathing out her last with an Et tu quoque mi fili.

Are not these, my Lord, very afflicting thoughts? And yet they are but the least part suggested to me by these dishonourable articles [of the Treaty of Union].

. . . The greatest honour that was done unto a Roman, was to allow him the glory of a Triumph; the greatest and most dishonourable punishment, was that of parricide: he that was guilty of parricide, was beaten with rods upon his naked body, till the blood gushed out of all the veins of his body; then he was sewed up in a leathern sack . . . with a cock, a viper, and an ape, and thrown headlong into the sea.

My Lord, patricide is a greater crime than parricide, all the world over.

… When I consider this Treaty, as it hath been explained and spoke to, before us this three weeks by past, I see the English constitution remaining firm, the same two Houses of Parliament, the same taxes, the same customs, the same excises, the same trading companies, the same municipal laws and courts of judicature; and all ours either subject to regulations or annihilations, only we have the honour to pay their old debts, and to have some few persons present, for witnesses to the validity of the deed …

Good God! What, is this an entire surrender! My Lord, I find my heart so full of grief and indignation, that I must beg pardon not to finish the last part of my discourse, that I may drop a tear, as the prelude to so sad a story.

3rd November 2006

When Lord Belhaven sat down after delivering his famous speech, his pomposity was pricked wonderfully by the Earl of Marchmont, who quoted the Book of Samuel: "Behold, he dreamed, but lo! when he awoke, he found it was a dream."

Sir John Clerk gives a sense of the more substantive arguments made by those on the pro-Union side of the House:

The country should be thankful that we can debate its future freely, thinking not of war against our English neighbours, but of a peace to be strengthened, not of separating kingdoms already joined together by nature and their crowns and various common interests but of improving the union that exists. We on our side can also congratulate ourselves that our speeches are not directed to catching the wind of popular favour but to investigating our country's real needs.

As befits good citizens, our task is to set aside personal resentments and partisan loyalties and consider how Scotland's strength can be restored, its security confirmed, its royal house placed on a firm foundation and assured for all time, its people's welfare promoted and protected. As for the ancient honour and glory of our kingdom, the best way to show that we care for these things is by working hard to preserve them.

But an opportunity is at hand which, as far as human wisdom can foresee, will ensure that the sovereignty so gloriously guarded by our forefathers will be passed on intact to posterity. We all here profess the same goal; we all say the good of our country is what we wish for, strive for, even scheme for. Yet we seem to approach that goal in quite opposite ways. The union which you say will ruin us totally we shall present as the base on which to build a more prosperous and altogether greater future.

There is no dispute about the union of crowns. To uproot it after one hundred years would mean destroying Britain. James VI's accession by right of birth to the throne of England had at least one good result: a peaceful subjection to his rule of a people long hated but never conquered by his own . . .

It has long been remarked that the kingdoms should have been joined at the same time as the crowns, for a hundred years' experience has taught us that the one union without the other is bad for Britain. Even the English, who are happier than we in enjoying the royal presence every day, find that happiness precarious in so far as we envy it. And as for us, we have suffered so much from the union of the crowns that we must either regret it entirely or wish the bond had been more firmly tied. But destiny decreed that Scotland should be an object-lesson to all kingdoms never to join their crowns without a full communication of privileges . . .

6th November 2006

Three hundred years ago today, anti-Union fighting broke out in Glasgow.

Trouble flared after the Rev James Clark, minister of the Tron church urged his flock in his Sunday sermon not to trust parliamentarians or princes, but to be "up and valiant for the city of our God!" The next day, the Lord Provost, John Aird, was surrounded as he walked through the town towards a coffee house and urged to draw up an address to Parliament objecting to the proposed Union on behalf of the council. He refused, although he indicated he would not object if someone else drew one up. Before long, a mob consisting of "young lads and women of no good lives", according to an eyewitness quoted by Michael Fry, had broken the windows of the coffee house, from which Aird had fled.

The principally Presbyterian opposition in the town was soon augmented, uneasily, by Jacobites. Two local men, Findlay and Montgomery, led an unsuccessful attack on the tolbooth in search of arms. Undeterred, they led a mob out on the road towards Edinburgh. They got as far as Kilsyth, where they waited for their supporters. Very few came.

News of this "uprising" led to 200 dragoons being sent out from Edinburgh. To avoid confrontation, Findlay and Montgomery led their mob south to Hamilton, but they found little support there either, and returned to Glasgow in time to be arrested by the soldiers who had arrived from the east.

The arrests did not spell an end to the rioting, however.

7th November 2006

In his next letter to his spymaster, Robert Harley, Daniel Defoe raised the issue of how the Church of Scotland was dealing with the Treaty of Union:

> In my last [letter] I hinted to you what the Church was doeing as to their address or protest against the Church of England constitution.
>
> . . . as to the general opinion it gains here I must own it does some harm – but not what it was expected, for while it was in debate, like the English fleet while it lay at Torbay it kept all France in suspence, so the country expected the Kirk would have protested as the Burghs have done against the Union in generall as destructiv to the civill intrest and the intrest of the church in general, but instead of that it contains six heads . . . all which suppose the Union as reall and certain.
>
> I had this day the honor to be in the committe of parliamt appointed to examine the drawbacks and equivalents and they have desir'd me to assist them. Their debates will end in makeing explications on the heads of excise and drawbacks and I believe I shall have the honor to form them I shall . . . I hope to be able to give

you a scheme of their demands ... I would be glad that after I send you a draft of the subject I might be instructed what will or will not be conceded in England, since it is so ordred that I am in their cabinet by some mannagemt and can influence them more than I expected ...

Now to lead them to anything which England will not complye with, or to put them off anything which makes a difficulty here and may be complyed with, is equally acting against the Union.

Their Lordships have resolved to committ the drawing up the explanations to me, and if directed I might do more service to both kingdoms than I could have expected. If therefore my service here be of any moment I shall beg to be instructed or if I take wrong aims to be excused.

Next post I shall transmitt a draft of the things in debate. I am, your most obedt servt, DF.

8th November 2006

When the Scottish Parliament convened to consider the Treaty of Union, many barons, freeholders, farmers and inhabitants of burghs complained that union had not been what would nowadays be called an issue at the time of the previous election.

They therefore sought to make clear to their representatives that they opposed union. They did so through a series of addresses which were delivered to parliament.

These addresses were ignored by Lord Queensberry and the Court Party as if, Lockhart of Carnwath said, they "served no other use than to make kites".

Many took the same form and were amended according to the particular requirements and demands of different areas. Here is an example of one signed by the inhabitants of 30 or so burghs from Dunfermline to Denny, Linlithgow to Lesmahagow:

To His Grace, Her Majesty's High Commissoner and the Right Honourable the Estates of Parliament, the Humble Address of ... Humbly Sheweth,

That we, undersubscribing, have seen the articles of the Union agreed upon by the commissioners nominated in behalf of Scotland, and the commissioners nominated in behalf of England, in which they have agreed that Scotland and England shall be united in one kingdom, and that the united kingdom shall be represented in one and the same Parliament. And seeing it does evidently appear to us that such an incorporating union as contained in these articles is contrary to the honour, fundamental laws and constitutions of this kingdom, Claim of Right and rights and privileges of the barons and freeholders and burrows of this kingdom and church, as by laws established, and that the same is destructive to the true interest of the nation. Therefore, we do humbly beseech your grace and Honourable Estates, and do confidently expect, that you will not allow of any such incorporating union, but that you will support and preserve entire the soveraignty and independency of this crown and kingdom, and the rights and privileges of Parliament, which have been so valiantly maintained by our heroick ancestors for the space of two thousands years, that the same may be transmitted to succeeding generations as they have been conveyed to us. And we will heartily concur with you for supporting and maintaining our soveraignty and independency and church government with our lives and fortunes, conform to the established laws of the nation.

9th November 2006

The only burgh to submit an address in support of the Union was Ayr, where, Lockhart of Carnwath observed, "they got one subscribed, but by so pitiful and small a number that they thought shame to present it, especially when one a little thereafter, against the Union, was signed by almost all the inhabitants of that town".

This view was not confined to the anti-Union side. Daniel Defoe, the English spy, said he discovered in the address "some seeming softness".

Why Ayr? It was a pocket burgh of the Earl of Loudoun, who was a key member of the Duke of Argyll's network (Argyll, a distinguished soldier known as MacChailein Mòr, or Red John of the Battles, had been enticed back from the war with France to help drive the Union through the recalcitrant Scottish Parliament).

Other members of the aristocracy attempted to follow Loudoun's example. "Yet", said Lockhart, "they could not, though they endeavoured to, persuade their vassals and tenants to sign an address for the Union, and were obliged to compound with them not to sign against it."

Despite the one-sided nature of the addresses, did they actually have any impact? They certainly caused panic in London, where the perception grew that the prospective Union could be in peril. Sir David Nairne, the Scottish Secretary-depute, wrote to the Earl of Mar, stating:

> I hope there would be as many and as good hands at them as at the other. It would have been of mighty use here, for I find people here, I mean coffee house company, begin to droop or despond to hear of so much doing against the Union without doors and so little for it.

Mar, who had tried and failed to organise pro-Union addresses, wrote back: "It is past time to get very many, and few would look worse than none."

Mar, Queensberry and Argyll held firm, arguing that parliament would decide, not the people. As Sir John Clerk of Penicuik said:

> ... although these addresses had been read in the house, they had no impact, because the will of parliament, strengthened by mature deliberation, was considered of more account than the voice of the people led astray by one faction or another.

Much later in the year, they grew more worried as a circular began to do the rounds urging subscribers to the various addresses to descend on Edinburgh and demand that Queensberry deliver a national address to Queen Anne, making clear their opposition to the Union.

But this failed because, once again, the Duke of Hamilton, ostensibly a supporter of such a national address, changed his mind. Shortly afterwards, a proclamation was issued outlawing "unwarrantable and seditious convocating".

10th November 2006

An Act of Security safeguarding the future of the Church of Scotland in the event of a Union was drawn up around this time. This would serve two related purposes: i) remove the main reason the General Assembly had for objecting to the Union; and ii) stop Kirk ministers from fomenting opposition by preaching against Union. Debate was, however, adjourned until the issue of supply had been resolved. Clerk of Penicuik takes up the story:

> This was almost an annual exercise, and so far the court party had been reluctant to burden the people in this way, lest parliament should seem to have been summoned for that purpose alone. but it has long been a matter of satisfaction to Scotsman that such taxes require the approval of the estates ... To challenge such impositions has always been opposition policy, since the government's strength depends on obtaining subsidies for the defence of the realm. So it would not have been surprising if opponents of union had tried to delay matters. But although no issue could normally arouse fiercer animosity, the outcome of this debate favoured the unionists, consent being given unanimously for the supply of an eight-month cess [land tax]. For the quick passage of this act two reasons can be found. The first was the opposition's tactic of not wishing to be seen to obstruct a royal command. The other was their hope that parliament would be dissolved once supply had been granted, especially in view of the persistent crying-down of union by the people. They could never believe that union supporters would hold firm to the end.
>
> At the next sederunt, debate was held up by the reading of petitions from some western parishes, mainly seeing union as a threat to the kirk that spelled spiritual death for the nation. It became all the more necessary to settle the church question quickly. Second reading of the Act for Security of Religion produced from some quarters the proposal of additional safeguards and from others the raising of captious questions and difficulties designed to sink union under a great show of care for the kirk. Amongst these was a stipulation that Scot be exempted from the English law requiring holders of public office in England to be Anglican communicants.

Justice ... demanded the insertion of a clause to that effect, since it would be an absurd anomaly for Scotsmen to be barred from holding offices in England under a union that offered full communication of privileges along with recognition of their church... Next came a plea that all public office-holders in Scotland should be required to swear that they sincerely regarded presbyterian church government as truly apostolic and that they would never try to alter it.

13th November 2006

When details of the Treaty of Union were first made public at the beginning of October 1706, there was an outcry in the Church of Scotland because no mention was made in these articles of the institution's future.

It was assumed that this spelled doom for the Kirk, which would simply be incorporated by the Anglican Church in the same way that Scotland was to be incorporated by England. All this just 16 years after the Kirk was restored to its position as the official church in Scotland following two centuries of religious strife.

Kirk ministers were instrumental in fomenting opposition to the Union – and its likely destruction of the historic Claim of Right – from their pulpits, and the General Assembly voiced its opposition.

Lord Queensberry and his Court Party realised that if they did not reassure the Kirk, they would never get the parliament to approve the treaty. "If we can but please the ministers in the security of the Church, our greatest difficulty will be over," wrote Lord Seafield.

The Court offered "perpetual security" to the Kirk's Presbyterian government in the form of the Act of Security, which promised:

> Her Majesty [Queen Anne], with advice and consent of the said estates of Parliament, doth herby establish and confirm the said true Protestant religion, and the worship, discipline and government of this Church to continue without any alteration to the people of this land in all succeeding generations; and more especially, Her Majesty, with advice and consent foresaid, ratifies, approves and forever confirms the fifth Act of the first Parliament of King William and Queen Mary, entitled 'Act Ratifying the Confession of Faith, and Settling Presbyterian Church Government'.

The Act was passed, by 113 votes to 38, on 12th November 1706, exactly 300 years ago yesterday. Its passing prompted the historian Michael Fry to note: "[It suggested] that to many Scots their Church meant more than their state."

John Clerk of Penicuik observed:

> The passing of this Act did something to calm the outcries of the mob and the fears of the clergy; in the churches, by and large, the trumpets of sedition began to fall silent. Ministers who had formerly meddled over-zealously in politics now learned to leave the direction of government to parliament. This greatly upset the Hamiltonians [followers of nationalist Lord Hamilton] who saw themselves abandoned by those they most relied on to stir up anti-union sentiment.

The Act of Security became an integral part of the Treaty – and in future all sovereigns would have to swear allegiance to it. From then on, it began to look as if Queensberry and Seafield would succeed in bringing about Union.

14th November 2006

The first article of the Treaty of Union, which enshrined the principle of incorporation, was passed by 116 votes to 83 on 4 November, 1706, although that decision did not bind Parliament: each article had to be approved for the treaty to be enacted.

Following the hiatus caused by the Act of Security, which safeguarded the future of the Church of Scotland, debate on the treaty resumed on 14th November on the second article. It concerned the succession.

To understand the background to this debate it is necessary to go back to 30th July, 1700. On that day, Prince William of Gloucester, the last of the future Queen Anne's 18 children, died at the age of ten. This, just 22 years after James VII and II had been deposed by William of Orange, threatened the Protestant succession.

Even though the future monarch would be Scotland's too, in 1702 the English parliament at Westminster passed – without consulting the Scottish parliament – an Act of Succession offering the throne in the event of Anne's death to Sophia, Electress of Hanover, who was descended from James VI and I, and her offspring. The newly elected Scottish parliament (1703) passed its own Act of Security which stated that Scotland would not accept the English succession unless freedom of trade and navigation were granted.

This caused consternation in England, among the Whigs in particular. They feared Jacobitism was rife in Scotland and that this would provide King Louis XIV of France with a platform for restoring the Catholic Stuart monarchy. Indeed, this was arguably the principal reason that England – which had hitherto been lukewarm about the idea of union – suddenly became very enthusiastic about it.

Article II of the treaty bound Scotland to the English succession and explicitly banned Catholics from inheriting the throne: " . . . all Papists, and Persons marrying Papists, shall be excluded from, and for ever able to inherit, possess, or enjoy the Imperial Crown of Great Britain".

Remarkably, the Court party managed to secure a vote in favour of article II. Why? The Jacobites were divided in their tactics and that duplicitous nationalist the Duke of Hamilton directed his supporters to back the succession while rejecting the other articles. Hamilton, it has been suggested, was hopeful that he himself might be crowned King of Scotland should the plans for union fail to succeed and the Jacobites fail to reimpose the Stuart monarchy on Scotland.

Clerk of Penicuik states: "The Jacobites were violently inflamed, pointing out to him [Hamilton] that they had hitherto opposed union to avoid a foreign successor, that only their King James had the right to rule Scotland."

15th November 2006

The era preceding the Act of Union bequeathed Scottish history some of its more unusual names, not least the memorable, Squadrone Volante.

This party – a much looser alliance than today's political parties – was named by a group of what the historian Michael Fry calls "flocculent young noblemen" who had recently returned from their grand tours with a "modish keenness for Italian culture".

As the name suggests, it was a "flying squadron" which, ostensibly, would vote on each issue according to merit, although it was broadly nationalist and in favour of the Hanoverian succession.

The Squadrone emerged in 1705 from the wreckage of Lord High Commissioner Tweedale's governing New Party, which had failed to impose any stability on the notoriously fissiparous parliament elected in 1703.

Argyll, who had replaced Tweedale as High Commissioner, dismissed the Squadrone as the "half a dozen", but in truth it carried four times as many votes – which it deployed tactically.

Clerk of Penicuik objected to it for proclaiming patriotism while "in their hearts they were known to have Court [party] preferments and places in the chiefest degree of veneration".

Yet it was to be instrumental in the passing of the Treaty of Union.

As Paul Henderson Scott observes, the Squadrone first demonstrated its usefulness to Queensberry's Court party on 15th October, 1706, when parliament voted on whether to proceed with or delay considering the treaty. Tweedale, Roxburghe, Rothes, Baillie of Jerviswoode, Marchmont and others in the group, who had hitherto been supporters of the nationalists Hamilton and Fletcher, voted in favour of proceeding.

It is possible, although it cannot be demonstrated conclusively, that they were offered a role in the distribution of the Equivalent money, Scotland's "compensation", although that certainly never happened. In any case, their mood seemed to be changing. Roxburghe wrote to Baillie: "If Union fail, war will never be avoided; and for my part the more I think of Union, the more I like it, seeing no security anywhere else."

Many were also growing increasingly convinced that Union would finally put paid to the prospect of a Stuart restoration.

Although a few of the Squadrone's members dissented, a majority of them voted in favour of the first article which enshrined the principle of an incorporating union.

From then on, they were supportive. Professor Christopher Whatley, in *The Scots and the Union*, states: "Squadrone votes proved critical in securing approval for several of the articles, which, had they been defeated, would have brought the union process to a shuddering halt."

16th November 2006

When it came to the debate on article three of the treaty, which proposed a single parliament for Great Britain, Lord Seton of Pitmedden, from the North-east of Scotland, an articulate advocate of incorporating union, argued in a famous speech:

> That the Union of Crowns with limitations on the successor, is not sufficient to rectify the bad state of this nation, appears from these positions founded on reason and experience.
>
> Two kingdoms subject to one sovereign, having different interests, the nearer these are one to another, the greater jealousy and emulation will be betwixt 'em.
>
> Every monarch, having two or more kingdoms, will be obliged to prefer the counsel and interest of the stronger to that of the weaker: and the greater the disparity of power and riches there is, betwixt these kingdoms, the greater influence the more powerful nation will have on the sovereign . . .
>
> This nation is behind all other nations of Europe for many years, with respect to the effects of an extended trade . . .
>
> My Lord, I'm sorry, that in place of things we amuse ourselves with words; for my part, I comprehend no durable union betwixt Scotland and England, but that expressed in this article by one kingdom, that is to say, one people, one civil government, and one interest.
>
> 'Tis true, the words, federal union, are become very fashionable, and may be handsomely fitted to delude unthinking people; but if any member of the house will give himself the trouble, to examine what conditions or articles are understood by these words and reduce them into any kind of federal compacts whereby distinct nations have been united: I'll presume to say, these will be found impracticable, or of very little use to us.
>
> But to put that matter in a clear light, these queries ought to be duly examined, whether a federal union be practicable betwixt two nations accustomed to a monarchical government? Whether there can be any sure guaranty projected for the observance of the articles of a federal compact, stipulated betwixt two nations; whereof the one is much superior to the other in riches, number of people, and

an extended commerce? Whether the advantages of a federal union, supposing it to be for the true interest of both nations? [Deploying historical examples, he suggests that the answers are no.]

In general, I may assert, that by this union, we'll have access to all the advantages in commerce . . . [and] good government, to improve our national product, for the benefit of the whole island; and we'll have our liberty, property and religion, secured under the protection of one sovereign, and one Parliament of Great Britain.

17th November 2006

Andrew Fletcher of Saltoun took exception to Seton of Pitmedden's speech, stating that it was difficult "when men are constrained to bring harm on themselves, harder still to give the finishing blow to this Parliament of ours, with whose welfare the lives and fortunes of so many have been intertwined, that we should hack to pieces this body, already grievously wounded, whose unworthy members we are".

He then moved on to address the substance of the third article, asking a question which was to resonate down to the advent of devolution in 1999: how, in a parliament of Great Britain, would Scottish interests be safeguarded when, compared with the vast numbers of English MPs, there would be so few Scottish MPs?

Without help or consolation we shall shed tears in vain, the English themselves will laugh at our distress, and the moral will be pointed that we brought it on ourselves.

The Duke of Hamilton suggested that Scottish MPs at Westminster, acting as a group, should be given the right of veto on any "matters essential and fundamental in the Union". As Michael Fry states, "perhaps not unlike the Scottish grand committee of the 20th century – but with a sting available in their collective tail.

The opposition attempted, unsuccessfully, to delay the debate on article three until article 22, which dealt with the constitution and the make-up of the British parliament and proposed that 45 Scottish MPs and 16 Scottish lords should travel to Westminster, had been considered.

THE PATRIOT

They wanted, at the very least, what Seton had so contemptuously rejected – a federal union. Clerk of Penicuik exposed the trouble with such a notion: "[What] never appeared in those speeches or in the pamphlets spread around at that time was any willingness to define how such a union could be adapted to the British situation. So great were the difficulties surrounding it that it was clear that in the end public opinion would detect the fraud and uphold the more sensible view that no form of federal union could be devised which would give Britain a lasting peace."

The Earl of Stair cited the example of federal Holland, a republic.

> But does not such a prospect [a republic] horrify all right-thinking men? It goes against our destiny, against our natures, against the way the British peoples have ordered their affairs from earliest times. And leaving that aside, what would Scotland be left with under a federal union? … [It] must either quite cease to exist or survive in a lamed and mutilated condition, shorn of its majesty, its functions, its rights.

In the end, the article passed by 30 votes, prompting the Earl of Mar to state that the Court party's hardest work had been completed.

20th November 2006

In his letter of 19th November to his spymaster, Robert Harley, Daniel Defoe was able to report that the third article proposing a single parliament for the whole of Britain had been passed – but his letter also informed Harley that the level of violence in the country was escalating:

> I have the satisfaction to write to your honr that the parliamt has now voted the third article by a majority of 30.
>
> I am not willing to fill you with the apprehensions of people here, nor am I very flegmatick on that head myself, and therefore when I shall tell you that the commissonr has been threatned with daggers, pistols &c. and now that the last two sittings being within dark he was insulted by the rable in the street at his return, great stones thrown at his coach, and one of the guards wounded – I yet shall add that I am of opinion his grace will go [through] with the matter.
>
> I confess I thought it an ill concerted measure that last night the commissioner drove thro' the town so hastily, the foot guards runing and the horse galloping, at which the mob hallood and the enemy insults to, thus, the commisr was run away &c. Indeed it betray'd too much concern but that is not my business.
>
> The church has not yet done, and tho' in the review I am defending her proceedings, which you will easily perciev Sir I do not that I like them, but to checq the ill use will be made of it in England, yet I doubt she will go on till no honest man can defend her.
>
> Addresses are now comeing in from the respectiv presbyteries in ordr to justifye the comissions first address, and as by the enclosed which is the first of them you will see the nature of them, so I doubt others will be worse yet.
>
> All the west is full of tumult. Glasgow is mad. I was goeing to see what I could do there but met severall of the honest people flying and all advised me not to venture, so I have much against my will playd the coward and made my retreat, but I think to go next week incognito if it be practable, onely to observ and be able to giv you exact perticulars.

The commissionr is come down from the house to day by daylight, where they have debated but not yet voted this fourth article [on equality of trading privileges]. They came down without any disturbance as I yet hear of.

The ministers are quieter here now than before but in the enclosed petition or address you have two in perticular who were here in the commission and have been in the country . . . two firebrands and who merit to be markt as incendiaryes of whose I actions I doubt I shall have occasion to give you farther accounts, and I wish they dont bring them selves to want her [Majesty's] mercy.

21st November 2006

On 20th November, 1706, the articles of the Treaty of Union were burned on the point of a pike at Dumfries. Those behind this act produced an account of their reasons which was read at the town's mercat cross at one o'clock "with great solemnity, in the audience of many thousands; the fire being surrounded by double squadrons of foot and horse; in martial order".

The crowd gave their consent by "huzzas and chearful acclamations". The account reads:

> We have herein no design against Her Majesty, nor against England, or any Englishman; neither against our present Parliament, in their acts or actings, for the interest, safety and sovereignty of this our native and ancient nation.
>
> But to testify our dissent from, discontent with, and protestation against the twenty-five articles of the said Union, subscribed by the foresaid commissioners; as being inconsistent with, and altogether prejudicial to, and utterly destructive of this nation's independency, Crown-rights, and our constitute laws, both sacred and civil . . .
>
> [W]e must say, and protest, that the commissioners for this nation have been either simple, ignorant, or treacherous, if not all three; when the minuts of the treaty betwixt the commissioners of both kingdoms are duely considered; and when we compared their dastardly yeildings unto the demands and proposals of the English

commissioners; who, on the contrar, have valiantly acquit themselves for the interest and safety of their nation.

We acknowledge it is in the power of the present Parliament to give remissions to the subscribers of the foresaid articles; and we heartily wish for a good agreement amongst all the members . . .

[I]f the subscribers shall presume to carry on the said Union, by a supream power, over the belly of the generality of this nation: then as we judge, that the consent of the generality of the same, can only divest them of their sacred libertys, purchased and maintained by our ancestors with their blood: so we protest, whatever ratification of the foresaid Union may pass in Parliament, contrar to our fundamental laws, liberties & privileges, concerning church & state, may not be binding upon the nation . . .

And so we earnestly require, that the representatives in Parliament, who are for our nation's privileges, would give timeous warning to all the corners of the kindgom; that we and our posterity become not tributary and bond slaves to our neighbours, without acquiting ourselves, as becomes men and christians: and we are confident that the soldiers now in martial power, have so much of the spirits of scotsmen; that they are not ambitious to be disposed of, at the pleasure of another nation.

22nd November 2006

The next subject debated by the Scottish Parliament was article four: free trade.

English legislation of the 1660s, which prevented the Scots from trading with the colonies; the "ill years" of the 1690s, during which there were a series of famines that killed thousands; and the disastrous imperial debacle of Darien, which had left Scotland in an economically parlous state.

The English establishment knew that this was Scotland's weak point. Indeed, one of the threats used by Queen Anne to force the Scots to the negotiating table to discuss a treaty of union was to impose sanctions on Scottish exports to England.

Therefore, while there was a great deal of angst about the principle of union, the security of the Church of Scotland and the prospect of the Hanoverian succession, very few politicians and traders objected to the terms of this particular article, which proposed: "That all the subjects of the United Kingdom of Great Britain shall, from and after the Union, have full freedom and intercourse of trade and navigation, to and from any port or place within the said United Kingdom, and the dominions and plantations thereunto belonging; and that there be a communication of all other rights, privileges, and advantages, which do or may belong to the subjects of either Kingdom, except where it is otherwise expressly agreed in these articles."

John Clerk of Penicuik observed: "This of all the articles seemed the most useful to Scotland, the most likely to prove beneficial beyond any that human wit could devise, and the least likely to occasion more controversy."

This did not stop Andrew Fletcher of Saltoun objecting. He claimed free trade between the two countries would not be beneficial because different types of trade were subject to different conditions. "What privileges are they talking about? Possibly the right to bring in treacle or that American weed called tobacco. But where do we find the money to buy these things and the ships to import them? And even if we do get them here, to whom shall we sell them? Every market in Europe is glutted with such stuff. Among the positively harmful fruits of free trade is the prospect of more lucrative employment in England . . . No, they are plagues rather, snares, fetters of gold that we shall soon regret . . . "

Given that Scotland's early economic success was largely founded on the tobacco trade with the American colonies – which brought great wealth, especially to Glasgow – Fletcher's cavilling was unfortunately misplaced.

The article was approved by a large majority – 156 to 19. Fletcher, according to Michael Fry, "flounced" out of the House.

23rd November 2006

As well as his letters to his spymaster, Robert Harley, Daniel Defoe produced, long after the union, a book entitled The History of the Union between England and Scotland. While this work was obviously a post-hoc justification of his behaviour, it illuminates much of what went on. Defoe observed in late November:

> The Lord Chancellor acquainted the Parliament, that last night, His Grace, Her Majesty's High Commissioner, in his return to the Palace, was insulted by a number of people of the meanest degree, with stones, which was a high affront both to Her Majesty's High Commissioner and to the Parliament; and therefore moved that the Parliament may give the necessary orders not only to find out such as have been guilty as actors or abettors therein, but to prevent [it happening again] . . .
>
> The first rabble had been crushed, as has been observed already, and the vigilance of the government had secured the Parliament hitherto; but the inveterate fury of the poor ignorant people, imposed upon by the popular arguments of the times, and those enlarged upon by the various pamphlets and speeches against the Union, which were spread among them, was very hard to be restrained.
>
> The Duke of Queensberry, the Queen's High Commissioner, received divers affronts in the House going to and from Parliament . . . [He] had received several previous intimations of designs to assassinate him; and several letters, some abusive and threatening, others promising, to give him caution to preserve his person; others pretending to inform him of the designs, the time when ... and the weapons by which he was to be murdered.
>
> Whether those were real tensions, or only attempts to amuse, and perhaps discomfit His Grace in . . . so weighty a work, was, I believe, never certainly known: but, whoever will calmly consider the temper of the people at that time, how inflamed by the artifice of a party, and how far they showed their readiness to have undertaken anything they never said transpired, to have broken off this affair . . . that no agent of Satan was found hardened enough to have committed that, or any like sort of villainy.

. . . [H]ad any such villainy been perpetrated, [the plans for Union] would almost certainly have all been lost in the confusion that must inevitably have followed.

Everybody will allow . . . that it was time to put a stop to this violence, and to restrain the headstrong multitude, those made bold and furious, lest they should, as in such cases is not uncommon, run on to more violent extremes; and therefore the Lord Chancellor ordered the Lord High Commissioner to represent it to the House.

24th November 2006

After article four on free trade was passed, parliament moved on from grand issues of principle to the nitty-gritty of the treaty of union. Article five related to the privileges granted and restrictions imposed on Scottish shipping.

Clerk of Penicuik succinctly summarised the opposing viewpoints, first those of the nationalists:

The priveleges this article grants us are in fact restrictions, curbs on our merchants' ability to carry on business. But perhaps all the rights we enjoy under the laws of nature and nations should be reckoned as privileges, in so far as we are able to enjoy them without damage to England's interests. No doubt we should count it among our blessings and privileges that we are allowed to draw water and kindle fire and breathe the same air as Englishmen. The previous article gave us free trade; this one ensures that we shall lack ships to carry it on. What else can we make of the stipulation that our merchants must register in London the ships they own at present if they want to share the rights of English shipping, and, what is worse, prevents them in future from chartering or building ships abroad? . . . What is the value of trading privileges that we are prevented from using? You will say we can get our ships from England, but any trade depending on English goodwill will be precarious indeed.

The unionists replied:

Anyone who examines this article objectively, unemotionally, rationally will acknowledge not only its essential fairness but its peculiar fitness to British conditions. When the English freed themselves from tyranny in the twelfth year of Charles II's reign, they determined to revive their flagging commerce, passing an Act of Navigation in 1661. This allowed English ships many privileges denied to those of other nations. The act had three principal aims. First, to promote navigational science. Second, to develop an import policy that would benefit the English rather than foreigners by restricting imports of what England could grow or manufacture for itself. The third aim was to encourage merchants to build their own vessels. The result of this today is that many thousands of Englishmen are employed in shipbuilding, rivalling even the Dutch. From the success of that industry their neighbours benefit, but the pleasure it gives us must be tinged with envy, and to dwell on it is useless unless we bestir ourselves to imitate their prudence, frugality and skill. It is not only wise but essential that we implement a similar policy for our merchant shipping. That we have so few ships is deplorable; that we have insufficient trade to fill them is more so; but the lesson ... is how much we need union with England.

27th November 2006

Of course, the great clashes over the question of a union between Scotland and England did not always lead to exciting cut and thrust in parliament. In his History, Daniel Defoe captures, for 27th November, 1706, the routine nature of much of what went on in parliament, this time in relation to article six on adjustments to be made to the excise duties on grain:

> The sixth article of union again read, and a proposal given in for adding the word drawbacks to both clauses of the said article, which was agreed to.
>
> And the said article as so amended was again read, as also the proposal ... in relation to oats and oat-meal, with the addition of a further clause, in these terms, and that the beer of Scotland have the like rewards and drawbacks as barley.
>
> And it was likewise moved that another clause should be added thereto, allowing the like premium or drawback on the exportation of oat-meal, as is allowed on the exportation of rye in England, and after debate thereupon, it was agreed that the sixth article with the proposal for amendments should be remitted to a committee.

Thereafter there was a clause offered to be added to the said sixth article in these terms, viz. 'but Scotland for the space of . . . years after the first day of May next, shall be free from, and no ways subject to the prohibition and restrictions made against the exporting of wooll, skins with wooll upon them, and woollen yarn, which by the oaths of the sellers and buyers shall be made appear to be the proper growth and product of Scotland, and spun within the same, which shall no ways be comprehended under any of the laws already made in England, or to be made during the space foresaid'.

As also, a clause in these terms, viz. 'excepting and reserving the duties upon export and import of such particular commodities from which any persons the subjects of either kingdom are specially liberated and exempted by their private rights, which after the union are to remain safe and intire to them in all respects'.

And sicklike, another clause in these terms, viz. 'that after the union all sorts of Scots lining, or any kind of cloth made of flax or hemp, be exported out of the United Kingdom, free of all customs or other impositions . . .' [They were then] remitted to committee.

28th November 2006

Most of the extra-parliamentary opposition to the Treaty of Union came from the south west of Scotland. It was fomented by the Cameronians, who had planned to organise a march of men on horseback, armed with guns and swords, from Hamilton to Edinburgh. However, they realised that to succeed in their aim of blocking the Treaty they would have to win the support of the opposition leaders in parliament, the Dukes of Hamilton and Atholl. Despite the expectation that he would support the venture, Hamilton asked them to delay, so only a small number of men gathered on the appointed day.

Lockhart of Carnwath was puzzled:

What induced the Duke of Hamilton to this measure I shall not determine. Some swore he was under capitulation with the Court. Others will tell you he was afraid to venture because of his estate in England. All I ever heard alledged on his behalf was that he thought the nation was by no means in a fit state for such an enterprize at

that time, because the English had sent their troops to the borders
and more forces would be wafted over from Holland, and so the
nation be undone and all that joyned cut in pieces. But others said
that by this argument all opposition to the Union was in vain, for if
the English had a mind for it, why, it must be swallowed down.
But, even supposing it were so, his grace ought to have advertised
his friends of it, before he had counteracted what had been contrived
by them. Others again maintained there was no such hazard in the
attempt, because England, being engaged in a bloody war, would
have dropped the Union rather than drawn on themselves a civil
war.

But supposing it otherwise, they thought Scotland might have defended themselves for some time, till France had counteracted the troops that were to come from abroad, especially since the nation was unanimous and cordial in the cause and not seven thousand standing forces in all Britain, of which those that were in Scotland were so dissatisfied with the Union that everybody knew, and the officers had acquainted the government, that they could not be trusted, nine parts of ten being inclined to joyn with those that opposed it. But to pass over these things, I may assert, that had not the Duke of Hamilton taken this course the Parliament had been at once sent a-packing and the projected Union demolished. In which case all those that had appeared most forward for it would have fled, having horses laid and always ready to carry them off from the danger they had reason to dread and justly deserved.

29th November 2006

Although the Act of Security guaranteeing independence for the Church of Scotland had curbed much of the opposition to union in ministers' sermons, public hostility remained high. In an effort to suppress the continuing violence, the government issued a "Proclamation Against all Tumultuary and Irregular Meetings & Convocations of the Leidges": It outlawed:

[T]he raising of tumults and making convocations within the Burgh, and the riotous and disorderly assembling and continuing in arms thereby insulting the magistrates, and hindring them in the execution of their office; . . . also the rising in arms, marching in formed bodies through the country . . . and entring into bonds, leagues, and associations, for prosecuting illegal and unwarrantable ends, be declared to be open and manifest treason, and the committers, abettors and assistants in such crimes and practices ought to be prosecuted, and may be punished as traitors to Her Majesty and her government.

We are certainly informed that in several corners of the realm, and particularly in our Burgh of Glasgow, and other places within the sheriffdom of Lanark, and in Our Burgh of Dumfries, and other places adjacent, people have presumed, in manifest contempt of the laws, to assemble themselves in open defiance of our government, and with manifest design to overturn the same, by attacking and assaulting the houses of our peaceable subjects, continuing openly in arms, and marching in formed bodies through the country, and into our Burghs, and insolently burning, in the face of the sun, and presence of the magistrates, the articles of treaty betwixt our two kingdoms, entered into by authority of Parliament.

Therefore we . . . command all, and every person who has assembled themselves in manner above mentioned, to lay down their said arms, and disperse themselves & peacefully and quietly to retire, and betake themselves to their several habitations and employments.

And we prohibit and discharge any assembling or convocating in arms in manner foresaid, certifying all that shall be guilty actors, abettors, or assistants in the convocating or assembling in arms . . . shall be treated and pursued as open traitors, and the pains of treason execute upon them accordingly.

[The authorities are given orders to] disperse and subdue the said convocations by open force, and all manner of violence, as enemies and open rebels to us and our government. And in case any slaughter, blood, bruises, or mutilation shall happen to be done and committed by our said sheriffs, and officers of our forces . . . we do hereby fully remit, pardon and indemnify the same.

30th November 2006

As November 1706 drew to a close, with the main principles of union agreed by the Scottish Parliament, opposition to the treaty began to wilt. However, even Daniel Defoe, in his *History of the Union*, praised the persistence of the nationalists in securing a series of amendments which gave Scotland a degree of administrative autonomy to complement the independence of the Church of Scotland achieved through the passing of the Act of Security:

> From article to article, they disputed every word, every clause, casting difficulties and doubts in the way of every argument, twisting and turning every question, and continually starting objections to gain time; and, if possible, to throw some unsurmountable obstacle in the way.

The consequence of this was making amendments to the articles; nor was it a small disappointment to them, when they saw the parliament willing to come into amendments; and when, by the prudence of the committee, appointed to make calculations, and examine those already made, it appeared, that their objections were either answer'd and confuted, or the clauses so rectified and amended, as that they had no more room to fasten any of their cavils... 'Tis evident, the design was to load the treaty with a multitude of amendments; among which some might be found, which the Parliament of England would scruple; or, at least, that it would be a precedent for the Parliament of England to consider the treaty, and make more amendments; which being to come down to Scotland again, to be considered here, would bring another sitting on of course; when, by delays, the time fix'd to the first of May might be elapsed, the season of the year advance, which hitherto had not favour'd them for the riots and tumults of the country; and, in this delay, they might find further advantages.

1st December 2006

Article 7 of the Treaty of Union was – no surprise here – one that exercised the Scots a great deal, dealing as it did with real life. It was about drink. More precisely, it was about applying the duties levied on alcohol in England north of the Border. This was met with stiff resistance because in general English duties were higher, and the Scottish duties were collected with less rigour. The Edinburgh mob, as you might imagine, showed great interest in the progress of this particular article.

Daniel Defoe, the English spy, was even asked to give evidence on English duties to the Scottish parliamentary committee established to deliberate on the article.

Michael Fry, author of *The Union*, notes that while "sybaritic Englishmen" order pints by taste (mild or bitter), canny Scots ask for 60/- or 70/- or 80/-, the numbers having been inflated in later times.

John Clerk, of Penicuik, observed:

> These duties provoked much strife, particularly since a case could
> be made that they would mainly affect the poor. No wonder then
> that opposition speakers sought to alarm the mob by stressing
> heavily that 'tippeny ale', the common drink of most of the people,
> would now be taxed at English rates and doubtless at the level of the
> best English ale. The English had two kinds of ale, first and second
> quality (or 'small beer'), made with different ingredients, while the
> Scots ale was of medium strength, taxed at two shillings sterling on
> the Scottish measure. The article did not specify what tax should be

levied on this medium-strength ale, possibly in the hope that it would be classed as small beer. To prevent future wrangling, and avoid leaving the matter to be settled by inn-keepers and excisemen, parliament decided to refer it to the select committee, instructing it if need be to draft an addendum . . .

After diligent inquiry the committee recommended the addition of a clause to the effect that the excise on liquors should be the same throughout the United Kingdom except only that the English beer barrel, containing 34 English and 12 Scots gallons, which now sells in Scotland for nine shillings and sixpence without tax or twopence sterling per Scots pint after tax, should not after union be liable to higher duty than two shillings sterling. An alternative motion was 'that the Scots ale which now sells for twopence a pint should be reckoned like the small beer of England and charged no higher excise'.

After a wide-ranging debate these two clauses were voted on and the first was approved, though many thought the second safer and better. The anxieties of the mob were allayed, if not removed.

4th December 2006

On 20th November, 1706, the articles of Union were burned at Dumfries. This affront to the political process was raised in parliament almost two weeks later.

In his *History of the Union* Daniel Defoe contested the claim that thousands of people had turned out to witness the burning:

> [T]hey were not near so many as was reported at Edinburgh, where they industriously enlarged those reports, to intimidate the party that was for the Union, and, if possible, to set the mob in Edinburgh to work again; but the guards there did their duty so effectually, that there was no more appearance in the street, tho' loud threatenings were made of it.
>
> As to the burning of the articles, it was true that a number of people being got together, did publickly burn the articles of the Union, as concluded at London, with the list of the names of the commissioners of the treaty, and did affix a paper upon the cross of Dumfries, which they called, Reasons for and Designs in Burning the Articles, &c. after having read the said paper from the cross.

This paper was afterwards printed, and the printer being ordered
to be apprehended, fled for it till the first heat was over, and then he
appeared again, and was not questioned for it . . .

But it is to be noted, that whereas the paper mentions squadrons
of foot and horse, and the report was of 5,000 and 7,000 people,
5,000 in arms that entered the town, and 7,000 in the hills to support
them; it was all rumour, the most that appeared in this action being
about 200, and these in no sort of military order or equippage . . .

Yet was this disorder improved to a great height, and particularly
as it was improved to make the government apprehend, the western
people were resolved to concern themselves in this affair, and to
take arms against the government; the parliament was very sensible
of this, and being very loth to have any force made use of, they tryed all
the methods possible . . . to take away all opportunity of assembling
together, by which the people might be drawn into the snare.

It is observable, that even, in the house, there appeared some,
who were very loth to have these rabbles discouraged . . . [But] the
Lord Commissioner [Queensberry] had real and direct information
of this affair at Dumfries, and of private emissaries gone abroad to
excite the people to take arms.

5th December 2006

Parliament now moved quickly through the remaining articles of
the treaty. Debate began on article eight, which was designed to
impose the same duty on salt in England and Scotland.

This, observed Clerk of Penicuik, was "thought likely to have a
strong impact on Scottish trade and especially on the poor and those
engaged in the fisheries"; both fish and meat were preserved in salt,
which was also a constituent of porridge.

The English taxed salt heavily, the Scots lightly. Indeed, to help
the fishing industry grow, the Scottish Parliament had several years
previously prescribed that herring, salmon and other fish caught
in Scottish waters should be preserved in Spanish or French salt.

In an amendment, it was agreed that "to reduce the burden on
merchant-importers of foreign salt, such salt should be cellared and
locked up under the joint custody of importers and excise officials,

and released to the importer as required, not less than forty bushels at a time, on receipt of security that duty would be paid within six months".

For home-produced salt, a seven-year grace period during which Scotland would be exempt from duty had been reluctantly agreed by the commissioners who drafted the treaty in London.

But the opposition, here led by Fletcher of Saltoun, pushed for an indefinite exemption. His underlying motive had less to do with salt than trying to break the Union: he knew that Westminster would not accept an indefinite exemption, and that if Westminster objected to any of the amendments agreed by the Scottish Parliament the whole treaty would fall.

The Earl of Stair, for the government, tried to assure the house that the details could be resolved by the new Union parliament, but Fletcher shouted: "Don't trust the British Parliament for that! Would the English majority neglect their overtaxed constituents and turn a ready ear to our necessitous begging? The house might be governed by factions; the kingdom might be in some sort of crisis. There is no certainty of our getting even what we have been promised, let alone other things which we leave to the discretion of the English. Any improvements we want in this treaty should be written into it now." The pair just stopped short of fighting a duel over the matter.

Clerk observed: "After this and similar outbursts a clause was finally approved that, after the said seven years, Scotland should remain exempt from the duty . . . and that, if the British parliament . . . should substitute a new tax, then the Scots would pay their share of it but receive an equivalent as provided for in terms of the treaty."

With these amendments, the article passed on 26th December.

6th December 2006

Article 9 of the treaty of union related to what Clerk of Penicuik describes as the "land tax". He puts a positive spin on the deal proposed here: "In the whole of this great transaction there were no terms more favourable to Scotland than these, since her commissioners had taken the utmost pains to make the burden on landowners as light as possible."

For every £2 million raised by the English, the Scots would pay £48,000, a ratio of 42:1. This would not change when taxation increased or decreased. Clerk said: "So the unionists thought that the Scottish tax would be very far from grievous, since they foresaw that the sum mentioned in the article would rarely be levied except in time of war or necessity, and that instead Scotland's share would become progressively easier as union brought the hoped-for increase in her trade and wealth."

The opposition declared that the Scottish figure should not exceed £36,000, but in the end the article was left unchanged. Articles 10, 11, 12 and 13, on what Michael Fry describes as "minor fiscal" matters, were also passed with little disputation.

Article 14 on the malt tax was controversial because malt was used in beer in Scotland, whereas hops were used in England. It drew forth a complaint from Fletcher of Saltoun that Scottish malt should be free of duty.

The exemption was agreed but only in time of war, and the article passed by 18 votes – the lowest approval given to any of the treaty's provisions.

7th December 2006

Three hundred years ago to the day, the Scottish Parliament began debating article 15 of the Treaty of Union on the Equivalent – the sum of money to be paid to Scotland in recompense for taking its share of England's debts.

Among the most controversial of the treaty's provisions, its acceptance gave rise much later to Robert Burns' ballad with its famous line about the Scottish parliamentarians having been "bought and sold for English gold", and Sir Walter Scott's observation that the "Parliament of Scotland was bribed with the public money belonging to their own country".

The article, says Clerk of Penicuik, "engrossed everyone's

attention, full [as it was] of difficult, controversial material which gave the parties ample scope to belabour each other with calumny and abuse".

I will return to this particular subject in the next article, but for now let's assess the sum of money involved.

The article specified the odd sum of £398,085 and ten shillings, but as well as future contributions to England's substantial debt (incurred during a series of wars with France and Spain), it was expected to cover the losses of the disastrous Darien expedition, salary arrears for civil servants, the currency switchover and some subsidies.

As the accountant J G Pittendrigh observes in an informative chapter written for Paul H Scott's *The Union of 1707*: "It would have sufficed to cover Scotland's debts. It would have sufficed to cover the costs of the recoinage. It would have certainly been sufficient to pay subsidies to the fisheries and wool industry. However, taken altogether, it was grossly deficient."

Particularly controversial was what was known as the "Arising Equivalent". The commissioners who drafted the treaty believed that the subsidies would increase as Scotland's revenues rose from the economic uplift of joining England. Of course, this did not happen for some time, and initially tax revenues actually fell.

Pittendrigh states: "One does not need to be an accounting expert to detect that the Equivalent was an exercise in financial illusion. The tempting-looking amount ... was supposed to cover liabilities and commitments, which are now seen to have totalled at least £710,000 (even ignoring Scottish public debts of £250,000). There was a shortfall of over £300,000. In the short term the losers were mainly the public servants and their widows and orphans who were left to beg for their back pay and pensions . . . "

The question, then, arises as to why the Equivalent was passed by 112 votes to 54. I'll supply the answer tomorrow.

6

THE EQUIVALENT

"... let it never be said the Scots sold and
subjected their country for gold."

Lord Hamilton

8th December 2006

The debate over the Equivalent led to another of those marvellous
rhetoric-rich speeches in the 1706 Scottish Parliament, this time
from the Duke of Hamilton, which meets Clerk of Penicuik's
description of the "calumny and abuse" heaped by each side on the
other:

> Is it not enough that we must lose our freedom – that dear and
> lovely freedom our fathers defended against all assaults – not enough
> that we must lose our parliament for ever, without also being subject
> to intolerable taxes to pay others' debts?
>
> O Scotland, ancient but impoverished kingdom, who would
> believe that you, who can scarcely meet your own obligations, would
> be coerced into meeting those of others, and especially those of
> England, the richest nation on earth, England that has always made
> a mock of your poverty?

How shall we explain this to our children? It will scarcely excuse us to make the proud boast that from our meagre resources we volunteered aid to an arrogant and enviably wealthy nation, a people so spoiled by good fortune that they hardly realise it . . . And the facts concerning this English debt are in any case well enough known. Most of it cannot be paid off for a hundred years. All these duties and taxes that England has levied have gone as interest-payments on a sort of mortgage which, without the approval of her creditors, cannot be redeemed until its term has expired. So it is not only we who shall be crushed by this debt: it will hang inexorably

around the necks of our children. And let us not be taken in by the foolish view that the English are rich enough to afford it. Even now they are waging an enormously expensive war [against France] and contracting new debts daily to pay for it. And despite their continuing shortage of money they will go on to wage new wars.

As for the . . . money . . . count it as the price of our freedom, a reward for betraying our country. Never believe in it as just remuneration for assuming England's debts, for nothing good or fair should ever be looked for from an old and bitter enemy. We beg you, we beseech you by the memory of our forefathers and the love we bear our children, let it never be said the Scots sold and subjected their country for gold.

So why did so many members of the Scottish Parliament vote for the Equivalent?

The answer is simple: many had been investors in the Scotland's ill-fated imperial adventure in the Darien isthmus of Panama, and believed they would have their debts paid off (some did, others were left to bear the burden). Others, such as Queensberry, also benefited directly from cash handouts.

So there is a grain of truth in Burns's line about the Scots being bought and sold for English gold.

11th December 2006

In reply to Hamilton in the debate over the Equivalent, the unionists accused him of pandering to the mob, as related by Clerk of Penicuik:

These provocative words might have strained our patience if we had not determined from the start to pursue a steady course, through riot and slander, toward our goal of a peaceful and stable Britain. Treating every gibe with contempt, we must hold firm to our principle of allowing no private interests whatever to interfere with those of the nation. It is to earn the thanks of posterity, not of the mob, that we have taken all this weight of odium upon us.

Meantime your objections must be answered. Bear in mind that in formulating this union our delegates took as a prerequisite of free trade that all Britons should pay as far as possible the same customs and excises. Otherwise English trade could be ruined by goods brought in from Scotland on which lower duties or none at all had been charged, and the English resentment which that would cause would put paid to union and spark off old hatreds anew. What is true of customs tariffs would be equally true of other forms of excise . . . Now, seeing that England carries a heavy tax-burden (mainly to enable her to pay off her debt at the end of the present war in Europe), and seeing that unions require both peoples to be equally taxed, it follows inevitably that taxes raised here must be applied to the same ends as those raised in England: to sustaining the honour and dignity of Britain as a whole and to paying off the national debt – whether incurred by England or Scotland is immaterial if it is in the national interest to pay it. But since equal taxes result from this union, nothing could be more just or right than that the English should grant us this Equivalent to compensate us for the extra burden we must bear. It is useless to pretend that we could meet Scotland's needs by taxation raised here. Without this payment we would lack the resources to exploit the commercial opportunities of union and be quite unable to meet any of our obligations . . . The sum of £398,085 is to enable us to provide for such necessities [food or clothes for the poor], and it comes to us from England, not as a favour but as ours by right, not as a random concession won by our commissioners but as the product of disinterested calculation, measuring our present levels of taxation against those that will obtain at the time of union.

12th December 2006

Daniel Defoe observed of the debate over the Equivalent, which was to be paid to Scotland to help it cover its share of the British national debt in a union, that it re-ignited popular antagonism towards Parliament:

[I]t was the hardest thing in the world, to make the people in Scotland apprehend it; not but that those who were more immediately concern'd in the debating it, understood it well enough; but it serv'd as a handle to rally the union, & the thing being rendred as intricate to the common people as possible, that they might be the more moved to oppose it; these ignorantly running away with a notion, that Scotland was to pay the English debts, began to rage at the treaters again, and cry out, they were sold and betrayed ... the aversion to it rendred it in a manner contemptible.

To bring Scotland in to pay the English debts! What was not Scotland poor enough already? Was this the advantage of the union!

It could not be suffered, and the treaters had betrayed them: such discourse as this was the subject of the common peoples conversation, and the answering them with the story of an Equivalent to be paid them, was to tell them something which they neither understood, nor entered into the examination of.

It would be very hard to describe, how this kind of discourse irritated the poor people, and how they were imposed upon the daily accounts spread of this new wonder, called the Equivalent, of which calculations were made publick, representing, that in a year Scotland would repay all the money advanced from England, by the increase of common customs and excises; & so after that rate, notwithstanding of the Equivalent, Scotland would be drawn into an entail of taxes for an hundred years, to clear off the vast debt of twenty millions, which England was now liable to ...

I can not but note, that by a due calculation laid before the Parliament, it was made very plain, that England would be so far from being re-imburst in a year . . . that reckoning the common interest of the money advanced in the Equivalent, with the medium of years in which great part of the duties the other people had calculated from, was to expire, the Equivalent advanced in money to Scotland would not be re-payed in ninety years. Yet was not all this able to allay the prejudices of the people, at the affair of paying the English debt, which they run away with so eagerly, and so universally raged against, that had not the rabbles been in good time crush'd before, and that so effectually, that they could not begin again, it was thought this ... would have influenced them to a more dangerous degree than anything.

13th December 2006

Following the debate on the Equivalent, parliament turned to consider how the promised money should be used, as related by Clerk of Penicuik:

> It enacted first that individuals should be indemnified against losses arising from the replacement of the Scottish coinage by the English, as provided for in article 16. Because of the shortage of coin in Scotland, the universally damaging remedy had been devised of accepting both Scottish and foreign coins at more than their intrinsic value, almost a twelfth part above their true worth in gold or silver. This excess was to be covered when coins were withdrawn from circulation. Secondly, shareholders in the company trading to Africa and the Indies were to have their money refunded at the usual rate of interest and within the year, after which the company was to be dissolved. This measure seemed harsh to the company's officers and was accordingly challenged.
>
> For a great many years (so the argument ran) we had clamoured for such a company, finally securing it under King William after long pleading on our part and much hostility and dragging of feet from the English. Since then, the company had cost Scotland dear in money and bloodshed [through the Darien disaster], but had withstood the threats and machinations of its enemies and survived to this day. To allow it to capitulate to the English companies would be a national disgrace.
>
> Now, in particular, with our trade supposed to increase under union, the nation might finally expect some return for all that the company had cost it. The best way of proving the advantages of union would be to let the company reap the benefit of this much-vaunted free trade. Without such organisations in place, our efforts to improve our trade would go for nothing, since they were in a sense the cradles of commerce. Under their auspices, merchants would be able to serve Scotland better, since they had no hope whatever of gaining admission to their English counterparts.
>
> These fine-sounding arguments were answered thus: It is true this company has cost us dearly – what is dearer to a nation than its wealth and blood? Nor would we deny that difficult births should

be actively fostered, except when they cause more trouble each day.

We ought to have misgivings about a company which has hitherto proved so unprofitable to its shareholders: roughly half of its capital spent already with no visible return, and the balance under threat, particularly in view of the uniform taxation that will be applied to every company in Britain after union . . . Article 16 passed with the added stipulation that officers presently employed in the Scottish mint should continue in office . . .

14th December 2006

The debates over the articles of the Treaty of Union took place in Parliament Hall, the cavernous centrepiece of Parliament House, which of course still exists, albeit now surrounded by the wrap-around classical facade of the architect Robert Reid, constructed in the early 1800s.

Parliament House was built in the 1630s, at the height of the troubles caused by King Charles I's attempt to impose a new prayer book and liturgy on the Kirk. The king's actions provoked riots in Edinburgh, and these culminated in the signing of the National Covenant asserting the primacy of the Presbyterian form of government in the Church of Scotland. This, in turn, led to the Covenanting Wars, the so-called 'Killing Time'.

The Town Council of Edinburgh was charged in 1632 with providing a new building for parliament, the Privy Council and the Court of Session.

It took seven years (from August 1632 until August 1639), although there is no record of it having exceeded the £10,555 raised by the council from borrowing (two-thirds) and by subscriptions from Edinburgh citizens! It was certainly built by a Scotsman, Sir James Murray, who was His Majesty's Master of Works.

Lord Cullen* describes its components: "[It] comprised a hall for Parliament and a jamb (wing) to the east. The gradient entailed considerable underbuilding but enabled a Laigh (low) hall to be provided beneath Parliament Hall. The Great Door of Parliament

---

* *Parliament House: A Short History and Guide*, by Lord Cullen.

House faced the yard beside St Giles [Cathedral]. The doorway was in Renaissance style with rusticated pilasters, somewhat similar to one at the Argyll Lodging in Stirling. It was surmounted by a pediment which displayed the royal arms flanked by statues of Justice and Mercy. Beneath the arms was the motto *unio unionum* (the union of unions)."

The hall in which parliament sat is 123ft long by 42ft wide. Although extensively refurbished over the years, including the introduction of magnificent stained-glass windows, it still has its original 40ft high 'open timber' roof which was built – using oak transported from the Baltic – by John Scott between 1637 and 1639.

After union, Parliament House was handed over fully for use as the Court of Session, which was appropriate because, as Christopher Whatley observes, "government ministers still exerted influence over the appointment of judges, and, for a time anyway, lawyers – notably Lord Milton and Duncan Forbes of Culloden, but also men in lesser legal posts – continued to play an important part in the governance of post-union Scotland".

15th December 2006

When the issue of Scottish representation in the British Parliament – article 22 provided for 45 MPs and 16 members of the House of Lords – reared its head again, there was an outbreak of strongly nationalistic sentiment among the opposition.

"The embers of [this] controversy," observed Clerk of Penicuik, "having seemed to die down somewhat in the preceding debates, now burst into flame, the whole house wracked with grief and indignation, patriotic fervour and partisan zeal."

The opposition leaders, at first, hesitated between attack and defence, but eventually, like so many "gladiators", they plunged in:

> That the die had been cast for Scotland, and her fate sealed for ever, all good men knew when they saw that this house had passed article 3 [that there should be a single United Kingdom parliament], nor can they recall that unutterable woe without tears and groans even today. So where do we stop?

Having crossed the Rubicon, must we wade deeper into crime? Have we so little sated England's greed and ambition by agreeing to this calamitous union of parliaments that we must also deliver a maimed rump of ourselves into the ambush that awaits us?

For that is what this article means: that we butcher and dismember the venerable body that so long and so honourably has sustained our monarchs' dignity and our country's freedom.

Even at full strength, we have rarely been a match for the English, so how shall a few of us resist them? Who will stand up for Scotland when the English see that her parliament, her glory and her bulwark, has been utterly demolished? And where shall we turn for help?

Must we carry our grievances and complaints to the parliament of Britain, and rely on it to settle our disputes and grant us every favour? She will prove an awkward and cruel stepmother, you may be sure, deaf and tight-fisted, ready to unsay and undo after union all she has said and done before. Were the parliaments to enter union with their full numbers intact, they might yet salve their honour and dignity. Otherwise we face nothing but ignominy and reproach.

Our opponents have told us that fair and equal terms are the basis of a true and perfect union. By what standard of fairness does the English parliament retain all its members, while this august body contributes a mere sixteen nobles and forty-five barons and burgesses?

We should learn from the English to be fair to ourselves, for if we betray our own interests as shamefully as this we shall not be thought worthy of sharing the government of Britain."

19th December 2006

While the nationalists vehemently opposed article 22, which limited the number of Scottish MPs in the Commons to 45 and the number of peers to 16, the unionists were unapologetic, as related by Clerk of Penicuik, who quoted the Earl of Stair's speech:

At the outset let us be clear that in their discussions with the English our commissioners made every effort to meet the wishes of this house. They therefore pressed hard for a body that would unite the full strength of both parliaments, and when that effort failed, for the best possible representation of ours. Sixteen from our nobility, thirty-eight from our barons and burgesses was the original English proposal, to which they clung so tenaciously that it took several days of public and private negotiation to persuade them to raise the latter number to forty-five. Why they would not raise the numbers further should be understood . . . First, they contended that each country's suffrage should be determined by its contribution to the revenue, though they were willing to allow us one twelfth of the seats in parliament in spite of our contribution only being one fortieth. This principle we opposed on the principle that it had never been applied in England, where certain counties return more members than their revenues warrant. Further, relying on the prospect of our revenues increasing with commercial prosperity under union, we argued that Scottish representation should be based on our estimated future contribution, not our wealth at present. But the English had a ready answer to that, namely that in certain articles, such as the ninth on the land tax, it had been agreed that levies on Scotland should never be increased beyond a fortieth part of the British total, and by the same count in article 15 that Scotland should be compensated for any increase in taxation that was required for repayment of English debts. Look at it as you will, they said, you will find Scotland's share of the tax burden fixed at not more than a fortieth.

Their second argument, which weighed with us most heavily, was that our resources would be drained by sending a larger number of delegates to England, since we would find it hard to pay the expenses of the number proposed . . . But you ask why the English would not reduce their numbers to parity with ours. In case of urgent necessity they would no doubt have done so, but they had not sunk so low that they needed us to tell them what to do. You cannot force your will on those stronger than yourself. In the flourishing condition of England today, who can imagine persuading fifty or so members of its lower house to give up their jobs and hand over their authority to others? Had such a thought even entered the head of our commissioners, union would have been done for, or I am much mistaken.

20th December 2006

The Scottish Parliament continued to meet over Christmas and New Year 1706-7. But for much of the time it was mired in the technical details of the Union, as Daniel Defoe noted in his observations on proceedings for 20th December:

The drawbacks [exemption from duties] proposed upon beef and pork to be exported, were now the subject of debate; it had been examined in the committee, and they finding, that 1. The English had no allowance made them on beef and pork cured for exportation and 2. That the quantity of beef and pork so salted, and exported out of England, or out of Scotland, was very inconsiderable, had reported that there ought to be no drawbacks upon the exportation of salted beef and pork ...

But when this came to be debated in the parliament, it was all unravelled again; some gentlement would have it, that Scotland was able to export great quantities of beef, salted and cured to foreign parts; nay, some had before carried it further, and in their arguing for a trade with France, had advanced what had never before been heard of, viz that Scotland should supply France with beef, as they have formerly been supplyed from Ireland, and proposed infinite advantages from such a trade.

But these gentlement were soon silenced, when it was examined a little, upon what conditions, and in what quantities Ireland was able to supply, and did supply, not France and our island colonies only, but were able to supply all parts of the world, where beef was generally exported; that at that thime beef in any quantity was to be bought, ready cured in Ireland, including the salt and the cask it was packed in, at a half-penny sterling per pound, and that England was so convinced of this, that they could export no flesh, but sent their ships generally to Ireland, to load beef for their islands, and that France upon all occasions, got their beef, if possible, from Ireland, for the victualling their Navys and merchant ships.

Again, that the cattel in Ireland were larger and fatter than in Scotland, and their quantity so great, that England was obliged to prohibit their being brought over thither, otherwise they would over run the three kingdoms with the quantity ...

... the Irish beef was exported cheaper than Scotland could afford it; it was therefore argued, that Scotland ought to have the drawback allowed on their beef, to encourage the exportation, and if possible, to set them upon an equal foot with Ireland, in the trade of exporting beef, which, tho' it was proved, was not probable, yet as the affirmative carried some possibility, and the negative seemed to be of no great con sequence, the members came in to it, and they passed together.

21st December 2006

Despite his role as an English spy, Daniel Defoe grew fond of Scotland and remained here until November 1708, long after the two countries had joined in union. He returned frequently.

He was constantly confronting ignorance and prejudice among his fellow countrymen about Scotland, as the following from his *Review* demonstrates:

To hear our people speak of Scotland, or of the Scots affairs or people, it would make a stranger think that this same place call'd Scotland was some remote country in the East-Indies, or about Madagascar, ... or somewhere very unfrequented, where very few people ever came, and from whence, like our news from Muscovy, things were very uncertainly related and our accounts from thence very little to be depended upon.

The learned gentlemen of this party, tho' skill'd in history, masters of geography, and have seen [a] great part of the world in their travels, they'll tell you that Scotland is a barren, uncultivated, desolate country; that the land is all barren, and will hardly maintain the people that live there. Nay, they will very learnedly ask sometimes if there is any mutton, or any beef, or any butter, or any such thing as milk in Scotland. The Highlanders they take to be a sort of monsters, and ask if they live upon roots and the barks of the trees. Never was more wild notions in the heads of our people here of the Caribees in the Gulph of Florida... than they have of this people. Nay, one but the other day, who is a man of letters and a man of history, seriously and for real information ask'd me what sort of

I could add a great many such as these, as the constant result of the most profound and mysterial ignorance that ever was yet found among such a knowing people, such as we pretend to be. From all which I see a great deal of room to confirm the first maxim I laid down to myself when I had begun to enquire of, and consider Scotland, its people and circumstances, viz that there are not in the whole world two nations, that stand so near, have so much concern with and interest in each other, that know so little of one another, as these two . . .

Gentlemen, if the Scots want money, I must tell you, they do not want manners; and one piece of humanity they are masters of, which you with all your boasted improvements are without, and that is, courtesie to strangers, in which they out-do even the French themselves … Scotland really is so far from starving her inhabitants from any real defect of the land that it cannot really be call'd a barren soil.

From *Defoe in Scotland: A Spy Among Us*, by Ann McKim.

22nd December 2006

After all the violent opposition to the Treaty of Union had been suppressed by the authorities in October and November of 1706, principally because many of the leaders of the mob had been imprisoned, there were few outlets for the still simmering public disgust with the plans.

But late in December those who had earlier delivered addresses voicing their opposition to the Treaty began to talk of travelling to Edinburgh to demand an answer from Parliament; Queensberry and the Court party viewed this as provocative and moved quickly to outlaw any such gathering, as narrated by Daniel Defoe:

Tumults and riots in the country had been tryed in vain, and the Glasgow rabblers were closs in the Castle of Edinburgh, mobs and rabbles in the streets had been supprest, and the guards did constant duty in the city, walked the rounds in the night, and kept the streets quiet, the meeting of heretors and fencible men, had been discharged by proclamation, and the clause in the Act of Security, licensing them to do so, had been repealed; so that now no room was left for violent methods, except by open and actual rebellion, and that had all possible provision made for it in the laws, and the Queen had ordered troops to the borders of England . . . in order to assist and support the government, in case of necessity.

The only pretence therefore now was this, the addresses . . . had been continually brought in against the Union from all parts of the Kingdom, answers were not given, nor expected to be given by the Parliament, but they lay before the Parliament for their consideration; and an address lying before the Parliament, is, by the nature of the thing, supposed to be under consideration; but the addressers pretending, that no regard was had to their addresses, pretend now to come all up to Edinburgh, to wait for, or rather to demand answers to their addresses; this was too bare faced a pretence not to discover its own meaning; and therefore the Parliament immediately agreed to the Proclamation, to discharge or forbid all such gatherings or meetings of the subjects, as unwarrantable and contrair to law . . .

It was expected by some people, that these tumults should have had great encouragement on the part of the church; and great pains were taken to draw in the ministers in several parts, to espouse the quarrel, and to appear with the people against the Union.

But the ministers, however they shewed themselves against the Union in general . . . yet they shewed no inclination to encourage the tumultuary methods, that the violent tempers of other people seemed to be precipitating the nation into.

26th December 2006

On 26th December 1706, the issue of the Equivalent was raised again in the Scottish Parliament, in particular the second clause which, as related by Daniel Defoe, stated:

> . . . after the Union, Scotland becoming liable to the same Customes and Duties payable on import and export, and to the same excises on all exciseable liquors as in England, as well . . . as upon the account of the encrase of trade and people, (which will be the happy consequence of the Union) the said revenues will much improve

beyond the before mentioned annual values thereof, of which no present estimate can be made; yet nevertheless, for the reasons aforesaid, there ought to be a proportionable Equivalent answered to Scotland; it is agreed, that, after the Union, there shall be an account kept of the said duties arising in Scotland, to the end it may appear, what ought to be answer'd to Scotland, as an Equivalent for such proportion of the said encrease, as shall be applicable to the payment of the debts of England.

Defoe observed:

This was only to oblige the persons appointed by the government to direct the Treasury of Britain, that an exact account might be kept, what part of the revenue Scotland was to be appropriate, and for which the Equivalent was to be raised, in order also to come to a certainty in the measures which were to be taken with the remainder; and therefore this needed little debate …

The third clause runs thus, and for the further and more effectual answering the several ends hereafter mentioned, it is agreed, that, from and after the Union, the whole encrease of the revenues of customs, and duties on import and export, and excise upon exciseable liquors in Scotland, over and above the annual produce of the said respective duties … shall go and be apply'd, for the term of seven years, to the uses hereafter mentioned.

This was a general referring to the particulars, to which the over-plus of the revenue of Scotland should be applyed, and this will also come to be discoursed of in its place, being here pass'd of course.

The fourth clause was, and that, upon the said account, there shall be answered to Scotland annually, from the end of seven years after the Union, an Equivalent in proportion to such part of the said encrease, as shall be applicable to the debts of England.

This clause could admit no debate on the Scots side, since, as they had agreed, by the first clause, to come into an equality of duties, this was capitulating in behalf of Scotland, that an Equivalent should be paid by England for so much of the revenues of Scotland, as should be applyed to the English debts, over and above what had been already stated in the Equivalent named in the former clause.

27th December 2006

After the heated debate on Scotland's representation in the new British Parliament, Scotland's parliamentarians moved on to discuss the privileges of the Scottish peers, as related by Clerk of Penicuik:

> The first of several addenda moved was that they should renounce the privilege of enjoying personal security from their creditors. Some grudging individuals were indignant that the nobility, under union, should have more and greater privileges than before, for previously all Scottish members of parliament had been equivalent except in title. The motion was meant to satirise noblemen who had been commonly seen as over-zealous for union, and so their enemies amused themselves with comments like this:
>
> > 'From now on, noble lords are not to be trusted in matters of business. They can borrow without shame to stuff full their tottering palaces, knowing that the law has made them free of their creditors. And how are the debts they have already contracted ever to be recovered, if the threat of a squalid prison is lifted? Removal of the penalty will seem to remove the obligation to pay. Is there then to be a new set of laws for the nobility, as there was at the time of the Roman conspiracies? And is this the privilege they covet so greedily, to be free of their creditors? Their creditors should be warned to look after their interests while time permits.'
>
> These taunts, however, though ferociously uttered, had very little effect on the peers, who clung more tightly than ever to the privileges they would have under union and were willing to give way in nothing.
>
> Then some of them moved that the whole estate of the Scottish nobility should have the right to sit covered in the British House of Lords when their affairs made it necessary, in spite of the fact that only sixteen of them could vote. Others doubted the value of this motion, foreseeing that the dignity of the Scots peerage would hardly be enhanced if disenfranchised members were willing to enter the chamber.

When finally that clause of the article was reached which gave English peers created before union precedence over Scots of the same rank, the Hamiltonians began to remonstrate:

'Have we not amply sated English ambitions by giving the vote to only sixteen Scottish nobles? Must all the others too be stripped of their honours and dignities?

'Think, my lords, of your ancestors, of their virtues, of the renown you inherit from their great deeds at home and abroad . . . will you trade certainties for uncertainties?'

28th December 2006

On the issue of the privileges of Scotland's peers, Hamilton continued thus, according to Clerk of Penicuik:

As soon as this nefarious union takes place you must lose [rights to honours and dignities] too and be reduced to slavery, poor bondsmen of the English, you who were free men and scions of a nobility unsurpassed in Europe.

God does not always grant us honours and dignities and riches for ourselves alone: sometimes these blessings are bestowed for the sake of our successors. Remember that, and be worthy of your children and defend their birthright, and let their credit be the greater that you were their fathers.

The definition of true nobility is this, that only the path of virtue leads to the summit of honour. So learn to despise false and ill-gotten greatness, and strive with all your might to fulfil your ambitions by any other means than this mercenary alliance.

You do not have the strength, you say? Ah, but you do, if you also have the will, for nature herself will show the brave and the active how to repair their fortunes and restore their country to the heights of its ancient glory. And meantime let the English learn more restraint in the use of riches; let those upstarts learn from us how true nobility can be won.

These grandiose words received a short answer [from the unionists]: Honours and dignities and all that men prize must yield to the good of the country and its people. As for the nobility of England, you wrong them by calling them upstarts. Many of their families came to Britain with William of Normandy; many were here before he came, and still to this day flourish nobly and honourably to the credit of England, and show that their Saxon lineage can rank with the most famous in Europe.

But if there are indeed new men among their peers, as there are among ours, call to mind that it was the counsels of such men, their service and their worth, that upheld the Roman republic. Lucky the race that can bring forth and rear such men every day.

With speeches such as these the debate continued almost until nightfall, with no pause for breath until the vote was taken and the article approved. The status of the Scots nobility was radically altered by articles 22 and 23, and it is hard to determine if the change was for the better or for the worse, since they both gained and lost many privileges. The reader must decide for himself, but we can tell from the recorded votes that they brought their losses on themselves: forty-five peers supported the motions and only twenty-three opposed them.

29th December 2006

In the wake of the Darien disaster, the Scots were keen to preserve the existence of the African Company and, indeed, the company itself made representations to parliament, as told by Defoe:

> [S]ome motions appeared in the house . . . against dissolving the African Company; it is confest, the company was a thing the nation had a very great concern in, almost every family in the kingdom having some share in the stock, and consequently in the loss, for it was reckoned no better: the historical part of that transaction does not relate to this place, but it may be proper to say a little to it, to introduce the true understanding of the vote.
>
> The company had been erected upon a general subscription of 600,000 lib. sterling, most of it subscribed in Scotland, upon which every subscriber had paid down a certain part of the sum subscribed, and was lyable at the call of the company, to be pursued for the remainder, and to pay it all in, as by the several Acts of Parliament . . .

Upon the miscarriage of the expedition to Darien, and the return of their ships, &c, the company was so discouraged and disheartened, that no new attempt either there, or any where else, had been so much as talked of, nor was any other payments demanded, the loss of what was already expended lying very heavy upon the nation, and particularly upon some families who could very ill bear it.

The design had so effectually miscarried, that the stock advanc'd was not only expended, but the company was brought very low, and was very far in debt upon the account of their said expedition to Darien, and the subscribers were always apprehensive of a call upon them of some further payment, to discharge the remainder due on the old voyage, or perhaps to form some new expedition, and this made some people so uneasie, that they sold their stock in the said company for trifles, only to be secured against further demands; in general, the interest in the said stock was come to so low an ebb, that people valued themselves little or nothing upon their shares in it, and when the first view of the union came on, and some thought one way of it, some another, they either bought or sold as their opinion of the union, and its prospect of success either increased or decreased; and indeed the publick expectation of the success of the union ran very low . . .

The proposal . . . was rejected . . . this being a publick Act granted by Parliament, the Parliament first securing every man his whole principal interest, from the very time of payment, had undoubtedly a power to rescind their own Act, and cause cease all the powers and privileges which derived from them.

9th January 2007

As the deliberations on the Treaty of Union neared their end, one of the most able yet controversial figures on the Unionist side, John Dalrymple, First Earl of Stair, died suddenly on 8th January, 1707.

He had been closely involved in the debates, most recently over Article 22 on Scottish representation in the new British parliament, right up until his death.

"Sometimes," this consummate lawyer complained of the

nationalists who objected to the paltry numbers of prospective Scottish MPs and Lords, "they complain that all our members are not to be admitted; at other times that a united parliament will cripple us financially, our delegates returning home penniless. So what remedy do they propose? "Surely the only way out of the dilemma is to limit our representation as the article does."

But it was as the chief instigator of the Glencoe Massacre of 1692 that Stair was to be remembered.

A one-time lord advocate, Stair had been made joint secretary of state for Scotland with Lord Melville in 1691 by King William, with whom he travelled around Europe, although he kept in close touch with events in Scotland.

It was in this post that he ordered Thomas Livingston, the commander-in-chief of the king's forces in Scotland, to stamp out signs of Jacobite rebellion, particularly in the Highlands.

A proclamation was issued which "threatened the utmost extremity of the law against chiefs who did not take the oath of allegiance" by 1st January, 1692.

McIain of Glencoe, head of a branch of the clan McDonald, was technically the only one not to sign, having set off to do so in Fort William and, having been told he could not sign there, ventured through a snow storm to Inveraray, where he arrived on 2nd January.

The sheriff, Sir Colin Campbell, returned to work on 5th January and eventually allowed McIain to sign. However, this was not accepted by the legal establishment in Edinburgh.

Stair ordered the massacre to make an example of the McIains. It was carried out by Campbells loyal to the king who accepted the McIains hospitality before slaughtering them on 13th February. The massacre caused outrage and continues to be regarded as one of the most horrific incidents in Scottish history.

Stair was blamed, and his political career never recovered, although he did become a moderately important figure in the Union debates.

John R Young says of him: "After it [Article 22 of the Treaty] had been finally approved on 7th January, 1707, Stair retired to his lodgings. He died suddenly in bed during the early hours of 8th January, 'his spirits being quite exhausted by the length and vehemence of the debate'."

10th January 2007

January 10th, 1707 was taken up entirely by debate on the issue of the sacramental test. Swearing this statement of the primacy of Anglican faith was a requirement for holders of public office in England, but in febrile Scotland Presbyterian sensibilities would have been affronted had this been imported with the Union.

Some members of Parliament suggested that an alternative, Scottish test be applied with the following wording: "I, A. B., in the presence of God, declare that I acknowledge the presbyterian government of the church as now by law established to be the only lawful government of the church, and that I shall neither directly nor indirectly attempt to subvert it or to alter anything in its worship, discipline or government."

Daniel Defoe takes up the story:

> The affair of the sacramental test . . . had been moved in the Commission of the [General] Assembly, and great endeavours had been used, to bring the ministers in, as objectors, and a formula like this [the oath above] had been proposed there . . . but it failed on their side.
>
> The ministers were, in the first place, not willing to meddle with things of that nature; and, secondly, as to the formula, many of the ministers gave their opinion, that they did not approve of imposing any oath, or acknowledgement of the Church, as a test of civil employment; and, to have an oath of acknowledgement to the Church of Scotland be a counter test, was a tacit approbation of the method practised in England, which they detested.
>
> Others again were of the opinion that the subjects of Scotland were already, by the Union, exempted from the sacramental test in England by two several clauses;
>
> 1. in that the subjects of both kingdoms were, by the fourth article of the Union, to enjoy equal privileges and encouragements; and

2. that, by the act for the security of the Church government, no oath was to be imposed upon the members of the Church of Scotland, contrary to their principles; in arguing the first of these, it was alledged that, if a subject of Scotland taking the sacrament in the national establish'd Church of Scotland, shall not be capable of any place of preferment under the government of Britain, as well as a subject of England; then, do not the subjects of either kingdom enjoy equal privileges; and lastly, it was argued, that, by the last Article of the Treaty, the sacramental test might be understood to be actually repealed, as contravening the equalities of the treaty.

Stalemate resulted. But the clause outlawing imposition of the English test in Scotland was approved, and the notion of a Scottish test was rejected.

11th January 2007

As the debate over the Treaty of Union came to an end, there were several loose ends to be tied up, but that did not take very long, as Daniel Defoe related:

The debate of the rank and precedency of the Heraulds, and of the quartering of arms, the standards and colours was a thing of no great consequence, nor could it be referred to any body better than Her Majesty; and therefore the dispute of this was not long.

The keeping the honours, as they called them, in Scotland, viz. the Crown, Scepter and Sword, was indeed a material point, at least, as it had been made so by some gentlemen, who had pretended to excite the common people with apprehensions, that they were to be carried away to England, as tokens of surrendering the sovereignty of Scotland to the English.

But, as no such thing was ever thought of in England, the proposal met with no opposition; and some people thought, that not only the ensigns of royalty, but the royalty it self, sovereignty and government of Scotland, remain as intire, as the same things respecting England remain intire, either kingdom voluntarily consenting to an Union of power, an Union of government, and of all things needful to preserve both.

The last article, respecting the abrogation of all laws, which might be supposed to contravene the Treaty, met with no opposition at all.

And thus this weighty affair was finished on the side of Scotland, contrary, I believe I may say, to the expectation of all the world, who were amazed to see a thing of that consequence, and with difficulties which seemed in themselves insuperable, so successfully brought to a close.

A thing which had been so many times attempted in vain; a thing which had so often been set about, rather in a show than design of uniting; and I think I may say, a thing that never was heartily set about on both sides before.

It had held the Parliament of Scotland a long, troublesome, a dangerous, and I must owne a very uncomfortable debate, step by step, and article by article, from the third of October to the fourteenth of January, with very little intermission, for never was business closer applyed, more strenuously push'd, or more vigorously opposed.

The work that remained (I mean to the Parliament) was but short, and I shall do little more than relate the fact, which will be found in the minutes of Parliament; and I shall set them down in their order, omitting what relates to private business, as not material here; since I can very ill spare room for any thing, but what relates immediately to the business, and agrees with the title.

12th January 2007

I began this daily series on the events leading up to the ratification of the Treaty of Union by the Scottish Parliament back on 3rd October, 2006, to coincide with the period of the final session of the Scottish Parliament 300 years ago.

It is a fascinating period in Scottish history. For the nationalists and romantics it marked a low point during which, as Robert Burns would later put it, Scotland was "bought and sold for English gold" by a parliament comprised of a "parcel of rogues"; for unionists and those of hard-headed disposition, it represented sensible, self-interested behaviour at a time of great national crisis following the Darien disaster and the seven "ill years" of famine in the 1690s.

It is certainly true that the spectacle of politicians being bribed – either with cash, compensation for their Darien losses, or the lure of high office in London – is not edifying.

It is equally true that Union was not immediately accompanied by the much-vaunted economic benefits predicted in parliamentary debate.

Yet, trying to put myself in the shoes of those politicians, I think I would probably have been on the side of reason and self-interest, for the following reasons. Very often the debate over the history of 1707 becomes narrow and parochial. Of course, Union was not inevitable, but seen in a much wider historical and geographical context – great power politics, the much greater power of the monarchy relative to parliament, Scotland's parlous financial position – the choice appears much more stark than is generally accepted .

It must never be forgotten that the Union was instigated by the English. Several previous attempts at the behest of the Scots to bring about Union, beginning with King James VI and I after he inherited the English throne under the union of the crowns, had failed as a result of opposition south of the Border.

England was in the midst of a major war with the France of Louis XIV, the biggest power in Europe, and determined to prevent the French taking over the Spanish crown.

Queen Anne, and King William before her, were desperate for Union with Scotland, in order to prevent Scotland (where pro-French Jacobites were prevalent, especially in the Hebrides and the Highlands) becoming a back-door route for a French invasion.

Modern Scotland is rightly proud of its democratic tradition: but so limited was the franchise that the parliament of 1707 was never likely to reflect the public will. Even if it had, parliaments were only beginning to assert their power relative to monarchs.

Finally, I'm sure the threat of invasion by England if Scotland failed to agree to Union served to concentrate minds.

APPENDIX I

The key players

DUKE OF QUEENSBERRY

James Douglas, the second Duke of Queensberry, was the High Commissioner in the Scottish Parliament between 1702 and 1707. As the Queen's personal representative in parliament it was he who steered the Act of Union through the Parliament. As reward for this he earned himself an English dukedom and the nickname 'the Union Duke'. During the passage of the Act he lived in Queensberry House, now part of the Scottish Parliament building.

EARL OF SEAFIELD

James Ogilvie, first Earl of Seafield, was Lord High Chancellor and as such presided over the debates in the Scottish Parliament during the passage of the Act. Although a former Jacobite he was a loyal supporter of the crown and did much to ensure that the Act was passed. In later years he came to regret the passage of the Act and tried to have it repealed in 1713.

EARL OF MAR

John Erskine, sixth Earl of Mar, was an enthusiastic supporter of the Union and was Secretary of State from 1705. He played a key role in winning over potential anti-Union members but became disaffected after the Union largely because of a personal sense of grievance and lack of preferment. He played a prominent part in the Jacobite rising in 1715 and ended his days in exile. His nickname 'Bobbing John' arose from his willingness to change sides when things were not going his way.

DUKE OF HAMILTON

James Douglas Hamilton, the 4th Duke, was a Jacobite sympathiser who was the nominal leader of the anti-union Country Party from 1702. His questionable behaviour at key points in the debates suggest that he was assisting the union cause in secret. He was made Duke of Brandon in 1711 but died in a duel the following year.

FLETCHER OF SALTOUN

Andrew Fletcher of Saltoun, the Member of Parliament for Haddingtonshire, was the principal opponent of the Act of Union for which he is for ever known as 'the Patriot'. He had supported the Revolution of 1688 but the idea of an incorporating union with England was anathema and he became the leading spokesman for the Country Party. His speeches (as reported by others) and his pamphlets are the best evidence we have of the philosophical position adopted by the anti-Union forces.

APPENDIX II

The eyewitnesses

LOCKHART OF CARNWATH

George Lockhart of Carnwath, a Jacobite sympathiser, was a surprise choice as one of the Scottish commissioners charged with negotiating with the Union. In the aftermath of the passage of the Act he wrote his *Memoirs Concerning the Affairs of Scotland*, published in 1714, in which he strongly condemned those whom he claimed were bribed to support the Union. He later served as a Member of Parliament for Edinburgh at Westminster and fled into exile in 1715 following the Jacobite Rising. He was killed in a duel in 1731.

CLERK OF PENICUIK

Sir John Clerk was a member of the Scottish Parliament who supported the Union proposal and served as a commissioner although he did have reservations about the country's loss of an independent parliament. He believed that Lockhart and others had painted an inaccurate picture of the negotiations and wrote his own *History of the Union* by way of refuting some of the claims. Written in Latin, it was not published in English until the 1990s.

DANIEL DEFOE

Decades before he found fame as a novelist, Defoe earned his living as a writer of pamphlets, many of which attacked the Government of the day. To keep himself out of jail he agreed to write supportive articles instead and also to act as the Government's spy in Scotland in 1706. As a Presbyterian he was able to win the sympathy of the Scots parliamentarians and thus convey their thoughts and plans to his masters in London. He wrote *The History of the Union between England and Scotland*, which was published in 1786, as well as many letters touching on events of the period.

APPENDIX III

Guide to the key sites

It is now three hundred years since Chancellor Seafield, the second most powerful man in Scotland, stood up in the Scottish Parliament and proclaimed: "Now there's ane end of ane auld sang." His melancholy statement marked the end of one of the most tempestuous periods in the country's remarkable history. Between October 1706 and March 1707 members debated and, after much turmoil both inside and outside parliament, approved the Act of Union between Scotland and England.

It was clearly a period when, in that famous phrase, history rattled over the points. Yet for many people these events remain deep in lost time, accessible only through rather dry history books. Don't be fooled. In Edinburgh, history remains on show to the visitor. The main locations for the events that were commemorated in the tercentenary year still exist. They have all been modified, some dramatically, others less so. But their essence remains, and a walk on the city's spine – the Royal Mile – will take you to them.

PARLIAMENT HALL

Reached via Parliament Square and tucked in behind St Giles Cathedral, Parliament Hall is one of Scotland's hidden treasures. As part of the Court of Session, it is, however, very much part of modern working Scotland. Built in 1639 in Scots renaissance style with a magnificent hammerbeam roof, the interior is almost exactly as it was (the exterior was faced off in the 19th century with classical screens), although the parliamentary benches on which the three estates – nobles, barons and clergymen – sat are no longer there. Instead, it is one vast space. The walls are festooned with portraits of the great and the good. In continuing tradition advocates, to give Scottish barristers their correct name, can be seen parading up and down discussing the finer points of their cases.

Despite the years, it is not difficult to imagine the dramatic scenes played out here as Scotland surrendered her sovereignty. In one view this was because, as the national bard Robert Burns put it, the "parcel of rogues" in parliament were "bought and sold for English gold". Indeed much of the money from the Equivalent, which covered Scotland's losses in the disastrous imperial adventure in Panama, as well as around £20,000 in what may loosely be termed bribes, was dispersed mainly among the nobles. The alternative view is that Scotland faced ruin and had no choice but to agree to England's terms and conditions. On my last visit I had no trouble imagining Lord Belhaven, who was opposed to union, making his outburst: "Good God! Is this an entire surrender?" (Followed by a hammy request for a moment to shed a tear.) Or the Earl of Marchmont, puncturing Belhaven's pomposity, with his quotation from the Book of Samuel: "Behold, he dreamed, but lo! when he awoke, he found it was a dream."

Parliament Hall is open to the public, free of charge, during normal working hours. Go in the afternoon, when if you are lucky the sun will beam gloriously in through the splendid stained-glass window which shows James V inaugurating the College of Justice in 1536.

EDINBURGH CASTLE

Right at the top of the Royal Mile, and visible for miles around, Edinburgh Castle has been at the heart of most of the great episodes in the nation's history. During the debates over Union, it played host to government troops who were increasingly called upon to keep order in the streets because the town guard wasn't up to the task. Following publication of the Articles of Union in early October 1706, the anti-Union mob rioted frequently. These outbursts of violence were often sparked by the Duke of Hamilton, the so-called leader of the anti-Union faction in parliament, as he made his way in his carriage down to his billet at Holyrood. On one occasion Lord Queensberry, as Lord High Commissioner the noble tasked by Queen Anne with securing Union, found his coach pelted with insults, reproaches and the "flooers o' Edinburgh", or excrement. Queensberry was later to receive death threats.

The Castle was also the scene of one of the most fascinating subplots of the Union negotiations. Since the departure from Edinburgh of James VI to become James I of Great Britain in 1603, Scotland's crown jewels – crown, sceptre and sword of state – had been stored there (apart from a short interregnum in the 1650s when they were removed to Dunnottar to prevent Cromwell seizing them). Among the public they remained a symbol of the fact that Scotland was the oldest sovereign nation in Europe, and there were fears that they would be taken to England after Union. Such was the clamour that an amendment had to be made to the twenty-fourth article of union in January 1707 to ensure they remained in Scotland. Hidden in a chest made of oak and iron, they were rediscovered by the writer Sir Walter Scott in a room at the castle in 1819.

The Castle is open from 9.30am to 5.30pm. Admission is £11 for adults, £5.50 for children over 5.

THE PALACE OF HOLYROODHOUSE

At the bottom of the Royal Mile lies the official residence of the Royal Family in Scotland. As hereditary keeper of the Palace vacated by James VI, rebuilt by Charles II and trashed by the mob after the final departure of the soon-to-be-deposed Catholic King James VII and II, the Duke of Hamilton had a grace-and-favour apartment at Holyroodhouse. Although ostensibly leader of the opposition to Union James, the fourth Duke of Hamilton was regarded as a duplicitous character who in the end failed to rally those behind his cause. That may be because he harboured the ambition of becoming King of Scotland. Queen Anne was the last of the Stuart dynasty, and although England had voted to accept the Hanoverian succession, the Scots only came into line during the progress of the Articles of Union. Hamilton later won renewed favour from Queen Anne.

The Palace of Holyroodhouse is open from 9.30am to 6pm (although closed from June 26 to July 7). Admission is £9.50 for adults and £5.50 for children over 5.

QUEENSBERRY HOUSE

Now part of the new Scottish Parliament, Queensberry House in the Canongate was the townhouse of the Duke of Queensberry (the family's principal residence was at Drumlanrig in Dumfriesshire). Queensberry was reviled for his role by most Scots. The behaviour of his son James for many people came to be seen as a symbol of his father's actions towards Scotland. While the Union was celebrated with pomp and circumstance in London on May 1, 1707, the mood in Scotland was sombre. "Why should I be sad on my wedding day?" was played on the town bells. Nonetheless, young James held a feast. So mentally ill was the heir to the ducal title that he was normally kept under lock and key. On this occasion, however, he escaped, caught and murdered a porter and roasted him on a spit.

See www.scottish.parliament.uk for details of opening times.

NATIONAL PORTRAIT GALLERY

On Queen Street, the gallery has on display paintings of most of the key figures in the Union debates, including that of pro-Union commissioner Sir John Clerk of Penicuik, author of a contemporary account of the events of 1706-1707.

Open from 10am to 5pm (7pm on Thursdays). Admission free.

Notes

1   PWJ Riley, *King William and the Scottish Politicians*, quoted in Christopher A. Whatley, *The Scots and the Union*, Edinburgh University Press, 2006.

2   Iain McLean and Alistair McMillan, *State of the Union: Unionism and the Alternatives in the United Kingdom Since 1707*, Oxford University Press, 2005, p.30.

3   Quoted in Anne McKim, *Defoe in Scotland: A Spy Among Us*, Scottish Cultural Press, 2006, p.27.

4   Karin Bowie, *Scottish Public Opinion and the Anglo-Scottish Union, 1699-1707*, Royal Historical Society and The Boydell Press, 2007, p.7.

5   Alan Bullock (ed.), *The Fontana Dictionary of Modern Thought*, Fontana, 1988, p.799.

6   McLean and McMillan, p.19.

7   ibid.

8   ibid, p.20.

9   Whatley, pp. 3-4.

10 McLean and McMillan, p.23.

11 T. M. Devine, *The Scottish Nation: 1700-2000*, Allen Lane, 1999, p.3.

12 Mark Kishlansky, *A Monarchy Transformed: Britain 1603-1714*, Penguin, 1997, p.44.

13 McLean and McMillan, p.60.

14 ibid, p.14.

15 Sir John Clerk of Penicuik, *History of the Union of Scotland and England*, Scottish Historical Society, 1993, p.187.

Bibliography

Bowie, Karin, *Scottish Public Opinion and the Anglo-Scottish Union, 1699-1707*, Royal Historical Society and the Boydell Press, 2007.

Clerk, Sir John of Penicuik, *History of the Union of Scotland and England*, Scottish Historical Society, 1993.

Defoe, Daniel, *The History of the Union of Great Britain*, Pickering & Chatto, 2002.

Devine, T.M., *The Scottish Nation: 1700-2000*, Allen Lane, 1999.

Fry, Michael, *The Union*, Birlinn, 2006.

Kishlansky, Mark, *A Monarchy Transformed: Britain 1603-1714*, Penguin, 1997.

McKim, Ann, *Defoe in Scotland*, Scottish Cultural Press, 2006.

McLean, Iain, and McMillan, Alistair, *State of the Union*, Oxford University Press, 2005.

Scott, Paul Henderson, *The Union of 1707*, Saltire Society, 2006.

Szechi, Daniel, *'Scotland's Ruine' – Lockhart of Carnwath's Memoirs of the Union*, Association for Scottish Literary Studies, 1995.

Whatley, Christopher A., *The Scots and the Union*, Edinburgh University Press, 2006.